YOUR STORY

FOR

GOD'S GLORY

A Christian's Guide
To Sharing Your Faith
With Confidence, Clarity, and Impact

By Mary Ann Mariani

Praise for
Your Story for God's Glory

Your Story for God's Glory is a game-changer for anyone seeking to authentically share their Christian testimony with impact and conviction. As a professional speaking coach, Mary Ann Mariani brings a unique blend of expertise in communication and a deep understanding of the transformative power of faith. Through practical insights and actionable strategies, this book equips readers with the tools they need to craft and deliver their testimony with clarity, confidence, and compelling authenticity. Prepare to be inspired, equipped, and empowered to unleash the full force of your testimony with *Your Story for God's Glory* as your trusted companion. This book is not just about speaking; it's about bearing witness to the transformative power of God's love in a way that touches hearts, changes lives, and glorifies His name."

Curt Hensley, Serial Entrepreneur and Board Member of Cru, Jesus Film Project, The Barnabas Group, and Think Forever

"We all know what it feels like to want to share our faith with others, only to have our hopes dashed due to intimidation, trepidation, or worry about how it's all going to go. In times like these, we need some help keeping our eyes up as we engage with others. That's exactly what Mary Ann Mariani does for us in *Your Story for God's Glory*. If you are like me and need practical steps, sound wisdom, and a friend to lead you into a new season of sharing your faith boldly, this instructive resource is what you need."

Erin Weidemann, bestselling author, and founder
of Truth Becomes Her and Legacy Story Academy

"*Your Story for God's Glory* goes beyond mere testimony sharing—it's a comprehensive guide to crafting a meaningful 'God Story.' With relatable examples and practical advice, this book helps you share your faith journey authentically. I appreciated the emphasis on prayer and the clear outline provided. Whether you're a seasoned speaker or new to sharing your faith, this book equips you with the tools to inspire others with your story."

Jim West, Co-founder of The Barnabas Group

"Are you a believer? If so, you need this book. It is for anyone, and everyone, as a simple, doable how-to on sharing *why* you have faith. Your story matters—every single part of it, because you have no idea how God will use it for good. And He will because He doesn't waste a thing."

Rechelle Conde-Nau, Of *Unabashed You*, podcast and blog

"Nearly 15 years ago, I met Mary Ann at one of her transformative workshops. Her book *Your Story for God's Glory* distills years of coaching and teaching into an invaluable companion for anyone eager to transform their story into a bridge of empathy and clarity that touches hearts. If you wish to turn your personal experiences with God into compelling narratives that deeply resonate, look no further. This book provides the essential blueprint you need."

Maria Keckler, Ph.D. Author of Bridge Builders:
How Superb Communicators Get What They Want
in Business and in Life

"*Your Story for God's Glory* has been instrumental in helping me effectively communicate the vision and mission of our ministry. Mary Ann's guidance, initially sought for crafting my personal story for a fundraiser, has evolved into a valuable resource for my role as Executive Director. The principles taught in this book have become my go-to framework for delivering impactful messages about our mission. Whether it's a new message or a story highlighting our impact, I consistently revisit the best practices outlined in this book. I highly recommend it to anyone seeking to enhance their storytelling skills and effectively convey their organization's mission."

Julie Dowler, Executive Director
CAPS Pregnancy and Medical Clinics

"*Your Story for God's Glory* is a transformative guide that empowers individuals to confidently share their unique stories and illuminate God's remarkable work in their lives. Mary Ann's expertise shines through as she guides readers in shaping their personal stories, fostering greater self-assurance and appreciation for God's divine plan. Whether you're reminiscing about the past, navigating the present, or envisioning the future, this book serves as a beacon of empowerment, encouraging you to embrace your identity as a cherished member of God's family. I wholeheartedly recommend *Your Story for God's Glory* to anyone seeking to enhance their storytelling skills and deepen their spiritual journey."

Bob Shank, Founder The Master's Program

*Your Story for God's Glory: A Christian's Guide to Sharing
Your Faith With Confidence, Clarity, and Impact*
Text copyright © 2024 Mary Ann Mariani
Published by Kingdom Presenters Publishing

Cover design by Danijela Mijailovic
Author Photo: Amy Gray Photography
Book Production and Publishing Services by Miramare Ponte Press

Paperback ISBN–13: 979-8-9887128-0-0
eBook ISBN–13: 979-8-9887128-1-7
Hardback ISBN–13: 979-8-9887128-2-4

Library of Congress Control Number: 2023913556

Foreword

"There is no greater agony than bearing an untold story inside you." —Maya Angelou

In our individual journeys, each of us holds a story uniquely crafted by God. Sharing these stories uncovers the depth of our connection to our Creator and to one another. Mary Ann Mariani's book, *Your Story for God's Glory: A Christian's Guide to Sharing Your Faith with Confidence, Clarity, and Impact*, shines as a beacon of light, guiding believers on a transformative journey to communicate their faith with love and purpose—with clarity.

In reading Mary Ann's advice, I'm transported to the writing of my first solo book, *Woman of Influence: 10 Traits of Those Who Want to Make a Difference*, and the realization that being an influential leader means "earning the right to be heard so that others are moved toward their best." That's the essence of Mary Ann Mariani's guidance.

I have found that Mary Ann possesses a rare gift—the ability to inspire and equip others to share their stories authentically. In *Your Story for God's Glory*, she imparts practical wisdom, gifting us with a roadmap to navigate the intricacies of sharing one's faith with L.O.V.E.: Listen to God First, Organize Your Story, Value Your Audience, and Enjoy Sharing Confidently.

I wish I'd had this book in my hands before I wrote my first book or prepared my first speech. Sixty books and hundreds of speeches later, I find her advice still relevant, inspiring, and timely. Mary Ann lays out the steppingstones that will help you identify and format your story in a way that reaches hearts, impassions souls, and enriches lives.

As my friend Sharon Jaynes, author of *When You Don't Like Your Story*, wisely said, "We can have a better story when we look through the right lens." This book can be that new pair of reading glasses that will bring newfound clarity to your story.

Your Story for God's Glory will give you the wisdom you need to organize the faith stories God has put in your heart with meticulous care. Each chapter can be a step towards greater clarity, from mapping your spiritual journey to considering your intended audience to bringing the vividness of your narrative to life.

The timeless instruction from the Lord in Habakkuk 2:2 calls us to "write down the vision (He has given us) and inscribe it clearly on tablets, so that one who reads it may run (act)" (emphasis mine). *Your Story for God's Glory* is an invitation to trust in the unfolding of our narratives.

Bestselling author Beth Moore captures the essence of telling your story: "Tell your story. Shout it. Write it. Whisper it if you have to. But tell it." Bestselling author Priscilla Shirer reminds us that "when you tell your story, you free yourself and give other people permission to acknowledge their own story, too." Mary Ann models their sage advice by sharing her story through these pages, but she also gives us the tools to share ours with clarity and courage.

May this book inspire and empower you to embrace and share the unique story God has written through your life. May your story touch the hearts of those who long to learn of His glory. As you turn the pages of this helpful, hope-filled resource, you and your story will become all that God designed it to be—AMAZING!

Blessing on your journey,

Pam Farrel, International Speaker, Bestselling Author, Co-Director of Love-Wise Ministries

Note from the Author

Dear Reader,

When contemplating sharing your story, you might find yourself hesitating, questioning whether your life holds enough substance or significance to inspire others. Perhaps you feel that your experiences lack the drama or intensity often associated with impactful stories of faith. You may even wonder if God can truly use someone like you to make a difference.

Let me reassure you, dear friend, that every life is infused with divine purpose and potential, no matter how seemingly ordinary. Even in its simplicity, your story carries the imprint of God's grace and love. It's not always about the grand gestures or extraordinary events; it's about the authenticity of your journey and the transformation that unfolds within.

Even if you haven't scaled mountains or faced life-altering challenges, your everyday experiences, joys, struggles, and moments of growth hold profound value. It's in the mundane routines, the quiet victories, and the small acts of kindness that God's presence is revealed. Remember, it's not the magnitude of the story that matters but the sincerity of the heart behind it.

God delights in using the ordinary to accomplish the extraordinary. Just as He used a shepherd boy to slay a giant and a humble fisherman to spread the Gospel, He can use you right where you are. No matter how seemingly unremarkable, your story can touch hearts, ignite faith, and glorify God.

So, if you've ever doubted whether your story is worth sharing or if God can use someone like you, I urge you to cast aside those doubts. Embrace the unique narrative of your life, for therein lies the beauty of God's workmanship. As you journey through these pages, may you discover that your story, no matter how humble, is a masterpiece in the making, waiting to be shared for God's glory.

With encouragement and belief in your potential,

Mary Ann

Dedication

To the faithful who are making ripples for Christ,
whose voices and stories the world needs.

How to Read This Book

Your time is valuable!

This book is comprehensive because I believe you deserve the best I have to offer. However, not all the content may apply to you or your situation right now. You can quickly and easily find real-life examples and practical advice to help you deliver your story in a clear, compassionate, and compelling way.

Here are some tips to help you make the most of this book and apply it to your area of interest or situation.

Tip 1: Start with the Introduction and Chapter 1

Gain an understanding of how the four guiding principles will enable you to share your faith story with clarity, confidence, and impact.

Tip 2: Focus on the areas most relevant to you.

Dive deeper into the chapters that resonate with your current needs:

- **Understanding God's will for you, your story, and your listener** (Chapter 2)

- **Determining your 5-minute testimony** (Chapter 4)

- **Outlining your story for easy understanding** (Chapter 5)

- **Structuring the details to avoid bogging down the story** (Chapters 6-9)

- **Inviting your listener to join God's bigger story** (Chapter 9)

- **Tailoring your story for your listeners** (Chapter 11)

- **Increasing your confidence, while maintaining authenticity** (Chapter 12)

Tip 3: Learn from others' examples.

While examples are scattered throughout the book, the last few chapters are focused on specific situations. These will be particularly helpful if you are:

- **Encouraging the next generation:** parents, grand-parents, and homeschoolers (Chapter 13)

- **Nonprofit or ministry leaders/staff**: Effectively casting the vision and mission of your organization (Chapter 14)

- **Marketplace leaders**: Integrating your faith story with a secular audience (Chapter 15, Chau's story)

As God provides opportunities for you to share your story for his glory, may this book serve as a continuous resource for instruction and inspiration. Use it to steward your testimony and make a difference in the lives of those in your community.

Table of Contents

Introduction

Your life story is unique to you. This story, your story, is a precious gift from God, and it holds the power to touch hearts, transform lives, and glorify Him in ways you may never have imagined.

Although we each possess a unique story of faith and hope, many Christians would admit they do not feel prepared or confident to share their faith story with a friend. Have you ever felt that way, like you weren't prepared to share your faith story with others? Did it cause you to hesitate, stumble, or feel inadequate to share—resulting in saying nothing but wishing you had? If so, you are not alone.

Let's start by taking the pressure off ourselves by realizing it's God's story we are sharing. Our story is the vehicle by which God chooses to make Himself known to our circle of influence. When we embrace that fact and allow Him to show us the way, then it changes everything.

You will know that your faith story has value—no matter what your faith journey looks like—when directed by God because He knows you and the needs of your listeners. He wants your story to have the ability to create Kingdom ripples that can make a lasting impact on others.

If you are reading this book, it's likely that you want to encourage others and make an impact for Christ. You just want a little guidance on how to do that in a way that authentically connects you and your message of hope with your listeners.

The good news is that there is a simple way for you to gain the confidence, clarity, and the ability to effectively share your story so that it connects with the hearts and minds of your listeners and introduces them to Jesus.

Welcome to *Your Story for God's Glory: A Christian's Guide to Sharing Your Faith with Confidence, Clarity, and Impact.* Within the pages of this book, we embark on a journey together—a journey that will empower you to embrace the extraordinary potential of your faith story and equip you with the tools to share it boldly, authentically, and purposefully.

But why, you might ask, is it so crucial to delve into the art of sharing your faith story? The answer lies in the profound impact it can have on both you and those who encounter it. Your personal journey of faith, with its twists and turns, victories and defeats, is a powerful testament to God's grace, love, and transformational power. When you learn to articulate and share this story effectively, you not only deepen your own faith but also become an instrument of God's love in the lives of others.

Throughout these pages, my goal is to be your guide as you navigate the beautiful but sometimes daunting task of sharing your faith. You see, I firmly believe that everyone has a story worth telling, and the message it carries can resonate deeply with others, leading them closer to God's embrace.

I want you to know that I am in your corner. I understand the hesitations, the doubts, and the fears that may have held you back from sharing your faith story in the past. But rest assured, together we will take that first step, and then another, until you find yourself confidently sharing your story in a way that truly touches hearts and changes lives.

Your Story for God's Glory encompasses the following key elements:

Confidence: Discover how to overcome self-doubt and hesitation, and to take steps of courage with the assurance that your story is a God-given gift to be shared with the world.

Clarity: Unearth the power of storytelling techniques that will help you communicate your faith journey with precision and impact, ensuring that your message is heard and understood.

Impact: Understand the profound Kingdom ripple effect your story can have on the lives of those who hear it, and learn how to make a lasting difference in the world through your testimony.

To aid you on this journey, you will be introduced to the L.O.V.E. guiding principles—an approach that will transform your storytelling and faith-sharing abilities. These principles are more than just letters; they represent a pathway to share your faith story effectively and from the heart.

Listen to God First: As Christ's followers, we want to seek God's perspective and guidance for us, our story, and our listeners. We want to ensure that His purposes are guiding our efforts.

Organize Your Story: We all know the struggle of trying to listen to a story that is not organized—it can be confusing and, at times, frustrating. Crafting a concise and compelling testimony story is a gift to your listeners.

Value Your Audience: A relevant story is compelling. It connects us as listeners at a heart level when we feel that the story has implications to ourselves. Personalize your story for your listeners, inviting them to become part of God's bigger story.

Enjoy Sharing Confidently: Audiences connect with real people, not perfect people. Nervousness often stands in the way of enjoying sharing your story. We'll look at how to manage those nerves when they show up so you can be yourself and enjoy sharing.

Through my coaching experiences with clients, these four guiding principles have enabled them to share their story confidently, stay true to their authentic voice, honor God, and engage listeners. Now you can use them to share your story confidently.

Why do I focus on principles versus a specific model or steps? You want the flexibility to personalize your story. Using guiding principles instead of a rigid model gives you greater flexibility to adapt in the moment to your specific listeners and respond to the Holy Spirit's guidance.

You also want this flexibility because your faith journey and your listeners will shift and change over time. You are in a relationship with Jesus, and because relationships grow and change over time, your faith story and how you tell it will also evolve.

To illustrate how these principles can work in real life, I'll introduce you to a few people whose stories I will reference throughout this book. These individuals, like you, have felt unequipped at times but have a deep desire to share their faith and inspire others. They come from diverse backgrounds and circumstances, yet their stories reflect the love and redemption that Jesus has given them.

- **Richard**: Vietnam veteran, grandfather, ministry volunteer

- **Laura**: Community Bible Study (CBS) Teaching Director, church volunteer

- **Oscar**: Former Gang leader—helps youth stay out of gangs

- **Becca**: 21-year-old college graduation speaker

- **Marcia**: Best-selling author and speaker

- **Ciara**: 13-year-old—shares rebellion story with parents and youth groups

- **Erin**: Cancer survivor, mom, successful entrepreneur

- **Chau**: Immigrant, business professional—shared faith story at industry conference

- **Jay and Shane**: Brothers, Young Life Ministry leaders—focused on foster care kids

As you can see, a variety of ages and backgrounds are represented here. You will learn more about these amazing people as you read on. What they have in common is the desire to honor God and to inspire others to greater hope and faith.

In your own unique circumstances, you may have a heart to share your faith story with family members, neighbors or co-workers, ministry volunteers, the unhoused, teens, or others. You may feel led to share with one person, a small group, or even a larger group. No matter whether you are talking to one person or many, the principles, ideas, and tips provided in this book will help you to share with confidence, clarity, and impact for the Kingdom.

God has uniquely equipped me to share these principles with you as your guide. I have spent the last 20 years as a presentation coach at 2Connect, an elite presentation training company serving top-tier multinational corporate clients. This experience with coaching executives to create and deliver presentations that connect with their audience and inspire them to action has given me a depth of knowledge from which to draw.

In 2008, I felt God calling me to apply my marketplace skills to Kingdom purposes. At that point, I started coaching people at my church who wanted to share their faith stories or communicate more effectively for their ministries. This grew to include working with other Christian organizations, nonprofits, ministries, and a wide variety of people who all share the desire to tell a compelling story that engages their listeners and introduces them to God's love and grace.

I have also sought out coaches and mentors, researched scriptures, and most importantly, I have prayed, asking, "Lord, I have these corporate skills, how can I bring *You* to the core of everything so that people see *You*, not just me, in what I am presenting or saying?" God has been faithful in showing me ways to accomplish that.

Interactions with clients and overcoming my own struggles with sharing my faith have influenced me to write this book. I desire to be obedient to God's call and to help you do the same.

If you desire to strengthen your faith and to share it with others—whoever God has put on your path in life—then you are in the right place. God wants to equip you to take steps of faith to make Him known. This book is a guide and a resource for equipping you to achieve that.

God first loved us. Our willingness to share our experience of Him through our faith story is a response to that love.

Let's prepare you to share Your Story for God's Glory.

Note: In the appendix, at the back of this book, you will find work-sheets and suggested exercises to help you implement the ideas shared throughout this book. Additional templates can be found at kingdompresenters.com/book-resources or by using the QR code below.

PART 1
Communicate with
L.O.V.E.

Chapter 1

Who Do You Say I Am?

One day, while sitting in a food court with my co-worker Ruth, the discussion turned to Christianity and the difference between faith and religion. We both had a background of attending church while growing up. The conversation pivoted to why we have the faith we have and how we decide who Jesus is in our lives.

I felt led to take the conversation a bit deeper and share my personal faith journey. Ruth was interested. I shared how, just a year earlier, I hit a low point in my life and asked my pastor why I struggled so much with trusting God with my challenges, even as a Christian. He responded, "Your faith was given to you as you grew up. You haven't really explored who Jesus is to you *personally*. You need to know Him before you can trust Him." I realized he was right. I had been practicing religion but was not grounded in my faith.

I shared with Ruth how I pursued reading the Bible, praying, and asking lots of questions until I learned the answer for myself. Once I did, I experienced Jesus in a new way—I began to trust Him, rely on Him, and understand the gravity of what He did for me on the cross. I was forgiven and redeemed from my past and able to enter my future with renewed hope and anticipation. I realized that the core of my faith is who I believe Jesus to be.

That changed everything for me. Then I asked Ruth, "Have you found who He is for *you*?" She wanted to think about it.

About a year later, Ruth told me that "Holy Spirit seeds" had been planted that day. She had a similar conversation with someone a few months later, leading her to enter a personal relationship with Jesus. I realized that this conversation would not have happened if I had not struggled with my own faith and been willing to share that struggle with her.

Jesus asks, "Who do you say I am?"

Jesus asked Peter that same question. *"Who do you say I am?"* He knew Peter must settle that in his own heart and mind before he could share who Jesus was with others, and also to be prepared to face the many challenges ahead for him.

We won't be confident sharing our faith story until we have wrestled with and answered that question in our hearts. This wrestling—the experience of determining who Jesus is in our lives—becomes our testimony story.

Peter could answer that question concisely and confidently because he had spent time experiencing who Jesus was and saw firsthand the miracles Jesus performed and His deity and character in action.

If you are a Christ follower, you have experienced Jesus firsthand, too. Maybe you experienced His love, grace, and salvation through a saved marriage, overcoming an addiction (drugs, alcohol, pornography...), surviving a reckless lifestyle, experiencing the blessing of a wished-for child, or a transformed heart.

We are each unique in our experience of Jesus' love and grace. We have uniquely gained hope, inspiration, healing, provision... or just the strength for another day from Him. Our path to reach the point of surrender and to accept Jesus as our personal Lord and Savior is unique to each of us. Your experience of Jesus' love and grace can provide hope to others.

If you are asked to give the reason for the hope you have, are you prepared to give an answer? If your response is "I'm not sure" or "not really," you are not alone.

Our fears and concerns may be valid, but they do not take away the fact that God has placed a unique story in you that has the power to encourage hope and faith and make an eternal difference in someone's life.

God asks us to be willing to share those experiences with others—to be willing to share our answered prayers, struggles, pain, healing, and transformation. That is what makes the experience of Jesus relevant to us and those who hear our story. We are asked to be prepared to share that hope with anyone who asks so that there will be readiness to answer with gentleness and respect.

"But in your hearts set apart Christ as Lord. Always be prepared to give an answer to everyone who asks you to give the reason for the hope that you have. Do this with gentleness and respect" (1 Peter 3:15, NIV).

If Jesus has given you hope, then you have the ability to share that hope with others in a way that can make Him known and transform their lives, as He did for you. The people in your circle of influence want and need to hear it from you, in your own voice, with your own unique story of answered prayers, struggles, and redemption, to believe it for themselves. You can show them how Jesus can and wants to meet their needs, too.

Someone made that difference for you.

Think about the person or individuals who most influenced your personal journey to know or love God more fully. What about them influenced you?

If you are like many of my workshop participants, those individuals likely shared their own personal journeys and how God helped them through their struggles. Chances are, sharing their story emerged from a genuine desire to encourage or mentor you.

Rarely do I hear that these people are famous, polished, or extremely knowledgeable about the Bible. In fact, they're typically ordinary individuals who were in the right place at the right time for God's use. Their personality, voice, and story were tools in God's hands to accomplish His purpose: to make Himself known to you.

We all can make that kind of difference. Yet, it can be a struggle to share your faith story in a way that clearly reflects what you feel about God, what He is doing in your life, and what He can do for your listeners.

So, what stands in your way?

God has called you to share the story of the difference He has made in your life. Yet, when asked to share your faith story, does your mind get filled with thoughts like these?

> *"What if I mess up?"*
>
> *"Where do I start, and how much should I share?"*
>
> *"Will I look stupid, judgmental, or like 'one of those people?'"*
>
> *"How do I talk about Jesus within my story?"*
>
> *"Who am I to share my faith story when so many people are more qualified than me?"*

It can feel overwhelming to figure out how to best tell your story in a way that captures the hearts and minds of your listeners.

What if I told you that you *can* have the courage and confidence to speak up because God promises to equip you? He is using this book as one tool to help equip you to answer His call to share the unique story of your relationship with Him.

Your story matters! Your voice can uniquely connect others with what God needs them to hear, know, and believe. Know that you are in the right place and the Holy Spirit is looking to prepare you to tell your story!

I want to help you learn how to deliver a compelling faith story so that you have the confidence and courage to step *up* so God can step *in* and make Himself known through you to anyone who hears.

My Own Wake-Up Call

I was asked to share my faith testimony at a women's event at my church. It would be my first time sharing my faith in a group setting. I prepared a 20-minute presentation of my faith story based on how I share information in the corporate work setting.

Then, I did a dry run with the pastor's wife to see what she thought. Of course, I thought she would like it and have a few minor suggestions. But her comments to me were not what I anticipated. She asked, "Where is God in your story? How will people know that it was Him who made a difference for you? How will you let our audience know He loves them and wants a relationship with them, too?"

Wow, I had completely missed the point! I had left the audience in the dark. I had not taken the time or consideration to share my story in a way that helped my listeners to know of Jesus' love, grace, and redeeming power. Of how He wanted a relationship with them, like the one I had come to know and love through my life experiences with Him.

This was a turning point for me. I realized it was an opportunity to seek God's guidance on how to share my story in a way that pointed to Him.

If you desire to strengthen your own faith and to share it with others God has put on your path, then you are in the right place. God wants to equip you to take steps of faith to make Him known. This book is a guide and resource for equipping you to achieve that.

Your Community is Waiting

God has given each of us a life to live and a story to tell. He asks us to share how He has impacted our lives with others in our community.

> *"Go home to your own people and tell them how much the Lord has done for you, and how He has had mercy on you"*
> (Mark 5:19, NIV).

Why is telling our faith story helpful to others in our community? Stories let people know God's grace is available to them, too. Sometimes, our best story of grace is that we are hanging in there despite doubts and disappointments. These stories of honest faith remind us to stay focused on Him—not our sins, failures, or problems, but on His promises. He tells us that nothing can separate us from His love. He promises to be with us and for us... and for those who hear of His grace and accept it.

You want to tell your story of grace, but like many people I have worked with, you may struggle to get to the point where you feel comfortable and confident enough to share it.

Let me introduce you to a couple of people, each with unique circumstances, who initially struggled to tell their story. They were willing to invest time and effort to learn how to share it in a way that ultimately impacted their community.

Journey to a Concise Testimony

Laura loves the Lord and has an amazing personal testimony. The problem is that it usually takes 45 minutes to tell it. Her story is complex and full of rich details, as well as the drama that often comes with a journey like hers.

In the past, it hadn't been an issue to take the time to share it. But more and more, as she ministered to women, she felt she was missing out on the opportunities to share hope and to build relationships because telling her story took too long. She knew there had to be a better way.

She asked me if I could help her pare her story down to ten minutes or less. As part of our process, I asked her what she wanted the listener to leave thinking about or focused on the most. After intentional prayer and reflection, she said, "I don't want them to focus on the drama in my life; I want to point them to the Savior in my life."

By shifting her focus in this way, she could let go of many of the details that led to a story of drama versus a story of a Savior. By getting her story to five minutes, she can now share it with more people and in various settings.

Tailoring for the Audience

I met Oscar when he was living at the San Diego Rescue Mission and participating in a rehabilitation program that helps the unhoused get back on their feet. Oscar had been a gang leader for over 20 years; his prior life was full of poor choices and a reckless lifestyle. He said, "I'm not sure how I lived this long. But I think it's because God isn't done with me yet."

When Jesus got hold of Oscar's heart, He put a desire in Oscar to help at-risk youth find a way to make better choices and not be pulled into gang life. Oscar wanted to use his faith story to help them see another way.

His target audience included junior high and high school students. The problem: We knew he had to grab their attention quickly! We needed to condense 20 years of gang life into a concise statement tailored to them. With that in mind, Oscar began with:

> *"I would like to share some significant numbers with you... 20, 15, and 2.*
>
> *20 is the number of years I have spent in prison*
>
> *15 is the number of felonies counted against me*
>
> *2 is the number of times I was stabbed; one in prison and one on the streets)*
>
> *I am here because I do not want this life for you! Some of you may think these are a Badge of Honor, but they are not. I wish someone had shown me a different way to do life—and that is why I'm here today—to give you some insights into this way of life and to offer you the option for a different life—one that is much better!*
>
> *I will share how I got here, the reality of living a gang lifestyle, and how you have options that can lead you to a much better life for yourselves."*

He quickly gained their attention and positioned the rest of his talk in a way that felt relevant to them. He recently had the gift of sharing his story at his stepdaughter's high school. His testimony encouraged her, and has opened the door to further conversations and opportunities to work with at-risk youth.

Six Minutes to Inspire Hope

Becca is the person God used to open my eyes to the transformative power of sharing our personal story with transparency, courage, and a belief that God will use it for good.

Becca had just been asked to give the valedictorian speech at her college. At 21 years old, she had very little public speaking experience. She felt anxious and wanted to make a good impression. She shared with me that she felt deep down she should share her personal story, hoping it would capture the significance of this moment. It was a brave choice. Her story involved traumatic experiences, hitting rock bottom, regaining hope, and overcoming many struggles to turn her life around.

The problem? She only had six minutes to do justice to the story and honor a collective moment with meaning for her fellow graduates. She felt honored to have this opportunity and wanted to represent her school and classmates well. She put in the work to deliver her story in a way that could be understood while also being concise and inspiring.

What impressed me most was her conviction to share her difficult journey to get to that day. She truly believed it would make a difference to the people in the audience. And it did! In the end, after receiving a standing ovation, hundreds of people approached her, saying, "I now have hope. Thank you!"

Jesus Makes Our Story Interesting

Nancy grew up in a small town with a loving family and a pretty normal life. She came to know the Lord in high school while attending a church youth camp. She loves Jesus and wants to share her faith but feels she does not have a dramatic story to tell and that people would be uninspired by her story.

Nancy is active in her church and community. She often has the opportunity to share her story and wanted some suggestions on how to tell it in an interesting way. I invited Nancy to reflect on 1 Peter 3:15 and think about what she would say if she was to give the reason for her hope. What was the unmet need or sin in her life that caused her to be open to hearing about Jesus in high school and keeps her in relationship with Him today?

Nancy first needed to understand it's Jesus who makes our story interesting. Sharing how He has redeemed us and met our needs connects our listeners to His love and grace for them. That makes our story interesting, even if we don't feel like it. Even though her needs may have seemed undramatic, she got in touch with the source of her hope in Jesus Christ. And from there, she could share her story with confidence and compassion.

Our stories do not need to be drama-filled or out of the ordinary to be inspiring. It's more about meeting our listeners where they are and inviting them into God's bigger story that has eternal value for them.

What About You?

These courageous people initially felt unqualified or unprepared to share their stories, but God had other plans for them. He knew they each had a special story that would resonate with certain people. They just needed some equipping to enable them to step *up* so He could step *in* and make an eternal impact.

We all have stories of transformation, redemption, and answered prayer. The question becomes, "Are you willing to be intentional with sharing your unique story with those God puts on your path?"

It becomes easier to say "yes" to sharing our story when we do it God's way—with Love. I shared the L.O.V.E. guiding principles at a high level in the introduction. In the following chapters, we will explore how to apply these guiding principles in various settings: Christian, non-Christian, one-on-one, or in a group.

Taking a Bigger View

You may intend to share your story one-on-one with people. Sharing your testimony with an individual is often the most personal and significant way to introduce them to the love of Jesus.

Yet, there may also be times when God prompts you to share your story with a group. Consider whether God is calling you to take a bigger view of the influence your story could have when shared with a group. One person who went from sharing with individuals to sharing with a group is Richard.

Richard had been thinking of how to share his testimony with his grandsons when an opportunity came up for him to share at his church's men's group. He decided to invite his grandsons to this event to hear his testimony.

By doing that, Richard gives us a bigger view of the value of preparing to share our testimony when opportunities like these arise. Here is what he felt his grandsons experienced at that event. Richard was:

- Willing to share his faith publicly; he showed them he was not ashamed to share Jesus with his friends.

- Intentional with his faith story: he prepared in advance to be concise, confident, and conversational.

- Connected his story to his listeners in a way that pointed to Jesus.

- Prepared for future one-on-one conversations with his grandsons and others.

Consider doing as Richard did; be intentional to prepare your faith story while remaining open to sharing it in group settings if given the opportunity. Ultimately, God will guide you to those He intends you to share your story with.

Creating a Kingdom Ripple Effect

How does a ripple begin? One drop... one question... one story that has the capacity to create movement creates ripples; when those ripples are for the Kingdom, they impact people's lives.

Most of us do not get to see the outcomes that a step of courage can have on another person. In my case, God has allowed me a glimpse into how He uses our faith stories to make a difference.

Ruth and I had that initial conversation 30 years ago. With God's prompting, I recently reached out to her and asked what was going on in her mind when we had that conversation and how her life has evolved as a result. Here is Ruth's response:

Ruth's side of the story

I didn't know it, but fear had a grip on me. When Mary Ann sat in front of me that day and asked me to think about who Jesus was to me, I was utterly stumped. I mean, what do you mean, who is Jesus to me? Literally, what do you mean? Then, as she talked about a personal relationship, again, I was stumped. I was like, Huh? What? A personal relationship? How's that even possible?

What I couldn't grasp at that point was the reality of a truly intimate personal relationship with, well, anyone! So, of course, I wasn't able to hold a sense of what that would be like with Jesus. I believed in Jesus; Jesus was the Son of God, but a personal relationship, like, huh?

That one question, that one confrontation with deep compassion, caused me to look in the mirror and honestly face a depth of fear of man that I had never come close to being able to acknowledge. To this day, I am living the life I live because of what Christ worked out in me through His forgiveness, His redemptive love, and His use of Mary Ann in that food court that one afternoon.

It would be easy to sit here thirty years on and give glory to God by listing out the ways He has blessed me and used me to impact the lives of others. Meeting the love of my life at age 42. Giving birth to our son at age 48 through the gift of embryo adoption. Making the way to owning a business where we strive to apply biblical principles in a way that will bring the light of Christ into the workplace. The list goes on and on.

But truly, what sits with me right now is not the answered prayer, accomplishments, or impacting the lives of others. What sits with me is the ongoing ripple effect one question can have on a person and how frequently we get in God's way by not asking the question.

The door to my heart began to earnestly open when Mary Ann invited me, with that one question, to reflect on who Jesus is to me. I'm eternally grateful that she did.

We all can make a ripple for the Kingdom with our story, questions, and compassion for those God puts on our path.

Dear reader, I believe you desire to add to these Kingdom ripples. Together, we can work to prepare you to start making your own ripples for those you care about.

For now, I invite you to continue reading and, as you do, reflect on your own story with Jesus. Know that *someone* in your community is waiting to hear your story.

Let's get you ready to tell it!

"Your brave may be someone else's breakthrough."
—Lead Pastor and Author Mark Batterson, *Win the Day*[1]

---

[1] Mark Batterson, Lead Pastor and Author. Quote referenced from his posting on Vimeo.com, November, 7, 2017.

PART 2

Listen to God First

Chapter 2

Discovering God's Will for Your Story

As Christians, we want to be good witnesses for God and make Jesus known and loved by those we come into contact with. That is why it's so important that we seek His guidance through prayer as we prepare to create and deliver our story. We want to start by listening to God first.

When we share our testimony story, we have an opportunity to communicate God's love, grace, power, and redemption. It's important to remember that even when we prepare our story, there is a far greater power at work than our mere human effort. We do our part when we pray and seek God's guidance, both in the moment and as part of our preparation.

We can't forget that prayer is a conversation. Like any conversation, we speak, we ask, and we listen. Starting our story preparation with a focus on what God wants to achieve is the best way to ensure that His purpose is guiding our efforts: It's His words, His love, and His purposes that allow our story to be heard.

When we pray to the God of heaven—the Father, His son Jesus, and the Holy Spirit—we are allowing our hearts and minds to be open to all that God has for us, our listeners, and our story. Our prayers are then embodying what Paul writes about to the Thessalonians.

"We always thank God for all of you and continually mention you in our prayers. We continually remember before our God and Father your work produced by faith, your labor prompted by love, and your endurance inspired by hope in our Lord Jesus Christ.

For we know, brothers and sisters loved by God, that He has chosen you, because our gospel came to you not simply with words but also with power, with the Holy Spirit and deep conviction" (1 Thessalonians 1:2-5, NIV).

God has chosen you to share your testimony with someone who needs to hear it. It becomes easier to know who that is and when to share if you start by seeking God's guidance. You also want to seek His guidance for how to make Himself known within your testimony.

When we operate in God's power and timing, amazing things happen! Trust Him to reveal that to you through your prayers.

Your Story is a Witness

Your story is a witness to how God is active in your life. When you acknowledge His role in your story, you are sharing the hope that you have in Christ—a hope that you want others to experience for themselves. His story is the part that makes a difference for us and our listeners.

God helped me understand this more deeply when He introduced me to Laura, the CBS Bible Study teaching director I referenced in Chapter 1. We believe it was a divine appointment. God was helping Laura and me learn more about Him and how He desires us to make Him known.

Laura and I first met at a women's retreat. In the weeks leading up to and following this retreat, Laura had been journaling her prayers and thoughts about becoming better at sharing her own testimony story.

Many months later, she realized how God had used our relationship and conversations as part of equipping her to share her story in a new way that was concise and pointed people to Jesus. Laura decided to send me a letter with her prayer journal entries so I could see God's hand in this for both of us. What a gift to receive and read this!

Laura has allowed me to share her letter and prayer journal with you because she believes it represents how many of us feel when it comes to the struggles of sharing our story in a way that gives glory to God, and the importance of seeking His guidance to achieve that.

In reading her prayer journal entries, she shares the importance of focusing on Jesus' role in the telling of our stories. Without pointing people to Jesus, we are not serving our listener in a way that leads to hope, faith, salvation, and eternal transformation. Her prayer journey also demonstrates how God is at work orchestrating people and events to help equip us to answer His call.

To provide additional context, I have included the opening of her letter, followed by five journal entries we felt would be valuable for you to read, each followed by its implication to help you prepare to share your own faith story.

Laura's Prayer Journal

Dear Mary Ann,

It is exciting to look back on my prayer journal and see how God had you and me running on parallel tracks and then POW! brought us together. Tuesday was, for me, a great confirmation of so much He has been telling me and calling me to do. It is remarkable to look back now and see how He has been moving and moving me toward this for a long time and I want to show you some of it.

I don't believe we'd met before I came to the orientation meeting for small group facilitators' orientation for the retreat. I had only signed up to take a small group because I knew if I didn't have that responsibility, I would find some excuse not to go to the retreat. I didn't know a lot of people and knew I'd chicken out.

At the retreat, the keynote speaker mentioned my testimony most unexpectedly. That night, at their request, I met with ten women in someone's room and told them my story. It took 35–40 minutes to tell it. I have told it many times, and God has used it powerfully for ten years, but this time it felt all wrong. Something was bothering me, even as I told it. The next morning, I awoke thinking about it and started to journal my thoughts and prayers. I want to share them with you because you are part of this journey.

<u>Prayer Journal Entry 1:</u>

My testimony has none of my sin in it! Only sad circumstances. I am an object of pity and compassion. No conviction of sin would be possible through hearing my story. The only result in a listener could be, 'Well, if she can be happy, I guess I can be." Is that the effect

I want my testimony to have? What do I want to leave them thinking about, asking themselves, considering about their own selves? Their need for forgiveness and restoration to God! It is only when we know our sin that we can know our need for a savior. Am I willing to share my sin? To share myself as a sinner? Am I willing to present myself as flawed? As more than admirable or pitiable.

Implication: We need to be willing to share our struggles and acknowledge our imperfections and sin. When we are willing to be transparent with our real-life struggles, that can lead to conviction in our listeners.

Prayer Journal Entry 2:

Lord, direct me in my walk with You. Who I was in the past was known to You and loved by You. And will be and must be used by You. May I not waste all that pain. The Spirit is talking through me to others. Mary Ann will help me prepare to speak. Get the confidence to get up there! God's timing, not mine.

The keynote speaker told me: "The story of your life is softening them and conveying God's love for you and letting them know that love is for them. That's the key. That is service." Add a conclusion in your testimony for your listeners. Our God is the God of hope.

Implication: God knows and loves who we were and are; that will never change. When we share, we need to do so confident of God's love for us. Grateful and excited that He can use anything in our lives to bring hope to others and to draw them closer to Him.

Prayer Journal Entry 3:

God, will You please prepare my testimony so it is done Your way? So it will give You glory and honor? So it will serve the needs of the audience? You had me tell my story at the retreat unexpectedly, and I woke on Sunday very unsettled by how it had gone. I thought a lot about it, thought of what it should be.

My story can be told as a mere saga to appeal to a human appetite for drama. And can do no more than lead to thoughts of me, not God. It bears no fruit that way. No glory to God. May it never be.

I have been thinking about it ever since. Days after the retreat, one of the women who heard my testimony asked me, 'So what was the turning point for you?' and I realized I had left them in the dark. Too many words.

Implication: We need to spotlight the key element of our story: the hope that exists in Christ alone, the forgiveness and new life that only He offers. God intends the circumstances of our lives to turn us to Him, and the sharing of our stories should clearly point to Him, too. Don't let Jesus get lost in a lot of detail or drama.

Prayer Journal Entry 4:

God, You are offering to train me in both testimony and outlining. Please do. I need You to teach me these skills. It will make me more usable for You. Mary Ann has scheduled a training at church. Perfect timing. (Mary Ann, this was the day before you approached me at church!)

Mary Ann asked me if I'd be a teaching example in her class. I offered to do a lecture, but she said it would be nice for me to share my testimony and asked if I could do a five-minute version of it. I initially panicked. I had been struggling with that, but I knew it was from God that I was asked to give it. Mary Ann provided some guidance ahead of the class to help me prepare. So, I wrote out a short testimony. And what a gift it was for me. To pare it down. To pare down decades of pain to a few words. What a relief. And to allow Him to be front and center.

Implication: We need to be willing to do what may be frightening to share our story effectively. God promises to equip, guide, and love us through the process.

Mary Ann, you thought I was doing you a favor. But God was preparing a great gift for me from your hand. Thank you for obeying Him in proceeding with your workshop. Not only the testimony part but all your teaching is exactly the help I have been praying for, for so long. Just the kind of organizational help I needed.

Thank you for asking me to be an example. It was a great, great day for me. This week has felt like the start of a whole new chapter in my life with Him. And in the way He will use me and my past for His purposes.

*"The Lord has done this, and it is marvelous in
our eyes" (Psalm 118:23, NIV).*

With love and thanks to Him and you,

Laura

I am grateful to Laura for being willing to share these prayer
journal entries with complete transparency, and for allowing
me to share them with you. It has changed my prayer life and
approach to organizing my own story. We hope it does the same
for you. Laura's five-minute testimony is provided in Chapter
15: *Steps of Courage*.

Praying for Your Listeners

As you seek God's guidance for your listeners, you have an
opportunity to add a different dimension to your normal prayer
life. It's an opportunity to think about and focus on what God
wants for your listeners and how that can shape your approach
to prepare a story that aligns with His purposes for *them*.

To better understand the concept of seeking God's guidance
while praying for our listeners, consider this analogy to a
conversation I would have with my boss seeking her guidance
for a new client engagement.

When I'm assigned a new client to help with their upcoming
presentation, I meet with my boss, Diane. In that conversation,
I ask her several questions:

- Who is this new client?
- What is the purpose of their presentation?
- Who is their audience?
- What are they concerned about?

- Why did they come to us?

- What do they most want help with?

- Why did you assign me to this client (versus another consultant from our company)?

I listen to her responses—often writing them down and asking clarifying questions until I feel like I have a good sense of how best to serve this new client.

What do you think would happen if I asked Diane one question and said, "Okay, thanks, I'm good?"

Bottom line: I would not be as prepared as possible to serve that client.

Yet, that is what I found myself doing when it came to asking God for help in preparing for my workshops or sharing my own testimony. I would ask one or two questions—more like petitions—but tended not to stay in the conversation long enough to learn His heart and will for my listeners and me.

Prayer coach Lisa Newmeyer[2], who has thirty years of studying, researching, and focusing on hearing the voice of God, opened my eyes to the fact that God desires to have the same kind of conversation with me as I do with my boss or friends. He wants me to bring not only my petitions and requests but the desire to stay in conversation long enough to learn His heart for me and the situation I bring to Him. By taking the time to ask, listen, and respond to Him in this way, I build a deeper relationship between Him and me and my listeners.

---

[2] Lisa Newmeyer, prayer coach and founder of Breakthru2u. For more information contact: lisa@breakthru2u.com

Lisa defines this kind of focused prayer as *Relationship Prayer*, and it's just another way to go to the Father with a heart to learn more about His love for us.

Through the practice of Relationship Prayer, I have learned that this changes my message and engagement with my listeners to be more relational than outcome driven. I have also learned that it helps with nervousness because it focuses on abiding in Him and doing His will, versus operating out of ego or fear.

God Speaks to Each of Us Differently

There is no right or wrong way to have a conversation with God. He speaks to each of us according to how He knows we hear Him best. How I hear God may be different from how you hear Him.

Some people hear from God in an audible voice, some see pictures or images of things, some hear sounds, some hear from God through worship songs or through Scripture. It doesn't matter how God communicates with you, just that you seek Him and allow Him to show you His love, grace, and will for you and your listeners.

Lisa reminded me that "it's not about throwing out the old or creating something entirely new with these prayers; you already hear Him because you are already saved. We are already in a relationship with Him."

We not only each hear from God differently, but we may address our prayers to Him differently based on our needs, situations, or preferences. Because we know that Father God, Lord Jesus Christ, and Holy Spirit, the three persons of the Godhead, are One, we may seek them in prayer separately or as One.

This is not meant to make it complicated, but to encourage you to get to know the different Persons of the Godhead. As you begin your prayers, know They are all listening, so pray what is on your heart.

The important thing here is to seek God's guidance in a way that honors Him and demonstrates a desire to align with His will and purposes for your story and listeners.

Learning God's Heart For Your Listeners

Relationship Prayer is similar to a conversation you have with a friend. When you make it personal and engage in the conversation longer, it can lead to a richer and more rewarding relationship. This type of prayer also helps you gain a greater understanding of God's heart and will for you and your listeners.

A good starting place in your prayer conversation with God is to acknowledge Him. Praise Him for who He is and what He is already doing in your life and those of your listeners. Ask Him to free your mind from any distractions and to fill you with His Spirit as you begin your prayer time.

This is how Larry entered into his Relationship Prayer time with God as he prepared to share his testimony with a group of young men.

> *"Father, thank You for caring for us. Thank You for caring for these young men who are losing their way, and want a new vision for their life. Father, may Your hand of guidance and Your Holy Spirit's presence be upon my testimony story and my efforts to speak for and about You. Father, I want to join You in the work that You are already doing in their hearts. I lift our time together to You. Father, please guide me."*

After acknowledging our heavenly Father and opening your heart and mind to hear His Holy Spirit guidance, continue to pursue the conversation with Him. Lisa teaches that it's helpful to ask questions, listen for the response, and write those responses down. She suggests keeping a journal of these conversations. It is rewarding to refer back to your journal and see how God was at work in your preparation.

It's important to understand that the actual questions you ask are *not* what is most important: it's the desire to seek God's love, will, and perspective. It is about establishing a primary focus on God and what He is doing with and through you and your story for your listeners.

Clients have shared that it was still helpful to have a few examples of questions to reference as they begin the practice of Relationship Prayer.

To get you started, here are a few examples of questions you may wish to ask our heavenly Father as part of seeking His guidance:

- Father, who would You like me to speak to about You?
- Father, how are You loving them? What is on Your heart for them?
- Father, what part of my story would You like me to share with them?
- Father, what would You like made known about You?
- Father, how can they best relate to You through me?
- Father, what is Your timing for sharing my story?
- Father, is there a Scripture reference for this?

Establishing prayer first is what Jesus did. He first listened to the Father so that He was aligned with God's will for the people, the situation, and the timing.

*"May the words of my mouth and the
meditation of my heart be pleasing in your
sight, O Lord, my Rock and my Redeemer"*
(Psalm 19:14, NIV).

Am I Hearing God's Voice or My Own?

I am not an expert in hearing God's voice; I can only share with you the personal experience I've had with my own prayers, along with what I have learned from Lisa Newmeyer.

Lisa told me a common question people ask her: "How do I know if I'm hearing from God versus myself?" I asked that same question when I first started intentionally spending time in prayer to seek God's guidance. Her response was, "The more we read Scripture, stay in our prayer conversation, and listen to Him, the more we come to know His voice separate from our own."

The analogy she shared with me is that when someone knocks at your door and you say, *"Who is it?"* the voice on the other side is either familiar to you or not. When you know someone personally, you can discern his or her voice. The same goes for our heavenly Father—the more we are in conversation with Him and read His word, the more we can discern His voice from our own.

*"My sheep hear my voice, and I know them,
and they follow me"* (John 10:27, KJV).

We also know that God never says something contrary to His word. One of the questions I always ask Him for is a Scripture reference. By looking up that Scripture reference, I see how the conversation is aligned with His word, and often find an additional perspective on the topic.

My friend and author Maria Keckler told me, "If you want to be on autopilot with your preparation, you better be bathing yourself in the Word. Because then His thoughts will be your thoughts. If I am a devotional reader, spending five minutes here and there, I cannot be trusted to be on autopilot. I have to intentionally stop to check in with the One who knows what a great story should be!"[3]

Dr. Dora Akietteh, in her *Heart of Prayer* workshop, talks about the power of prayer in preparing us to speak. She says, "Prayer transforms ordinary words into supernatural words. Prayer transforms our words into a dynamic power through which God works in our circumstances."[4]

By seeking God's will through prayer and studying His word, you are enabling the Holy Spirit to guide you in your efforts to share your story with eternal impact.

Seeking God's Perspective After You Have Shared

It's human nature to wonder how things went after you've finished sharing your story, especially if the response is different than anticipated. This is another opportunity to go back to the Father and ask what *He* did while you were speaking.

Consider asking Father God:

- Father, what happened as a result of sharing my story?
- Father, what did You do during this time?
- Father, how do You feel about what happened?
- Any other questions you have for the Father about this.

---

[3] Maria Keckler, Ph.D. *Bridge Builders: How Superb Communicators Get What They Want in Business and Life. New York:* Morgan James 2016

[4] Dr. Dora Akietteh, *Heart of Prayer* workshop; November 15, 2022, San Diego, CA.

Trust that if it benefits you in keeping with His will, God will show you what has been accomplished. Only know that He may reveal that to you in His own time and way.

Continue to ask God what your role is in the relationship with the person or group you've shared your story with. It may be the role of a "seed planter" or something else. What's important is to continue to go back to the Father to learn His purposes for you amid this relationship.

> *"My message and my preaching were not*
> *with wise and persuasive words, but a*
> *demonstration of the Spirit's power, so that*
> *your faith might not rest on men's wisdom, but*
> *on God's power"* (1 Corinthians 2:4–5, NIV).

Some people find it helpful to see an example of a Relationship Prayer to help them get started. I've provided two examples based on clients I personally prayed for as part of our working together.

The challenge with sharing these examples is that I am sharing a transcript of my conversation with God, not a suggested script to be used. Given that, please understand what I heard from the Lord made sense to me in the moment but may not make complete sense to you as a reader. I did not always hear from the Lord in full sentences and at times asked Him for clarification. My hope is that these examples will still provide some insights for you.

Example: Relationship Prayer for San Diego Rescue Mission Workshop

Context: I was asked to deliver a workshop for the San Diego Rescue Mission for people experiencing homelessness. These participants were just completing the yearlong program and the

Rescue Mission wanted to prepare them to effectively share their story at graduation and into the future. This is an example of the prayer conversation I had with the Lord prior to preparing to deliver the workshop. I began with acknowledging the Lord and then sought His guidance.

> Lord, I exalt you. You have provided for these brave men and women. You are providing a fresh start to a new life founded in You. They can now leave the old self/old man behind and embrace a new self in You. A fresh start! Lord, I seek Your guidance and Your perspective as I prepare for this workshop. You alone know what they need.

Immediately, Ephesians 4:22-23 came to mind. *"You were taught, with regard to your former way of life, to put off your old self, which is being corrupted by its deceitful desires; to be made new in the attitude of your minds; and to put on the new self, created to be like God in true righteousness and holiness.*

Therefore, each of you must put off falsehood and speak truthfully to his neighbor, for we are all members of the body."

As I read these verses, what I had not noticed before was that verse 4:23 focused on speaking truthfully to our neighbor (revealing the truth of our lives and God's redeeming nature). We are all members of the body who can benefit from this truth.

Below are the questions I asked to seek further guidance from the Lord:

Question: Father, what are You doing in this grad class?
Answer: (I heard/the Father showed me) Setting free, removing chains, giving voice to what is possible.

Question: Father, what is Your heart for them?
Answer: Love them, set them free, encouraging and equipping them.

Question: Father, how do You want to equip them?
Answer: SDRM set a firm foundation. Remind them they still need to learn, grow, and lean in and trust me as they step out.

Question: Father, what is my role to join You in that?
Answer: Encourage them—perfection not required to build hope and faith. Keep it simple.

Question: Father, anything specific (to teach or emphasize)?
Answer: No need to be perfect. There is no right or wrong way to tell their story. Let the spirit guide them.

Question: Father, any additional Scripture to reference?
Answer: Jeremiah 29:11, *"For I know the plans I have for you, declares the Lord, plans to prosper you and not to harm you, plans to give you hope and a future."*

I left my prayer time with an added focus on an attitude of encouraging them as much as equipping them.

Example: Marcia Ramsland: Christian Author and Speaker

Context: I met Marcia at a professional Christian women's networking event. When she learned what I do for a living, she told me, "I could use someone like you." I responded, "Great, tell me about you." She shared that she is a speaker and the author of the *Simplify Your Life* series of books (over 100,000 sold). My initial comment was, "How can I help? You're clearly a veteran at communication." She shared that she was about to speak at the Thelma Wells *Ready To Win Women's Conference* in Dallas. It's a stadium conference for 6,600 attendees. Marcia felt this was taking her speaking to a whole new level of influence, and she wanted to ensure that she delivered with excellence.

Before meeting with Marcia to discuss her presentation, I sat before the Lord and asked Him the following questions to gain His perspective for coaching her.

> **Question:** Father, what are You doing in Dallas on May 22? (The date of the event.)
> **Answer:** Singing My (God's) praises, filling them with joy, and preparing them for what's next.

> **Question:** Father, how can Marcia help in that?
> **Answer:** Help her audience to let go and embrace Me. I'm calling them to let go of what is routine, to break new ground.

> **Question:** Father, what specifically will help that?
> **Answer:** Have them realize they can't finish everything before creating space for Me (God).

Question: Father, is there something I am to share?

Answer: Focus on spiritual aspects versus tasks. Think of Martha and Mary. Simplifying life made it easier to sit at Jesus's feet when He was there. Scripture for simplifying life.

Question: Father, tell me more, I don't understand as it pertains to Marcia?

Answer: It's not about the talk or the curriculum she is sharing, it's about the attitude we need to adopt.

Question: Father, is there a Scripture for this?

Answer: Isaiah 42... simplify, peace, joy. God is the covering for it all.

"Sing to the Lord a new song, His praise from the ends of the earth" (Isaiah 42:10, NIV).

Question: Father, is there anything else to consider?

Answer: The Lord also impressed on my heart that Marcia has a platform to bring people closer to God, but she is not leveraging it. She should rearrange the storyline to give glory to God first, before the organizational process that she is known for.

Sharing this prayer with Marcia during our coaching session:

Marcia said this validated a similar feeling she was having with this particular presentation. She wanted to shift the focus to be more about God versus the organizing tasks she normally spoke on. Rearranging the storyline with this focus in mind allowed her to step into a stronger message that the audience resonated with: "Simplify your life with a spiritual decision first, and then your outside priorities will begin to take shape."

Marcia also decided to hand out a "Gospel tract" she had written to each participant to accompany her presentation. It anticipated this question: "But what if I keep working hard to get organized and I still feel stressed? Is there another way to simplify my life?" Her answer: "Yes, there's one way to clear the stress inside: with a spiritual clean sweep." Then, she included a prayer for the reader to ask Jesus to be the Lord of their life inside and out.

Her audience left inspired with a renewed focus on creating a place for God in their hearts as part of their daily plans and with a handout as a tool to help do that.

This chapter has focused on the power of prayer to discern God's will for you, your story, and your listeners. Seeking His guidance first provides you with direction for your testimony, influencing your story and its impact on your listeners.

With a clear understanding of God's heart and purpose for your story and listeners, we can now focus on why organizing your story leads to greater engagement and impact in Chapter 3.

PART 3

Organize Your Story

Chapter 3

Why Organize Your Faith Story?

We have all been there. You are listening to a friend or sitting in an audience, and you begin to wonder, where are they going with this? Or, what is the point?

Which leads you to mentally check out or, worse yet, get frustrated!

This is often a consequence of the person failing to organize their story. You don't want to be *that* person, right?

Without proper organization, your story may become confusing, hindering the impact you can have on your listeners. When your story is organized, it becomes easier for your listeners to follow along and connect with it.

Organizing your story helps you and it helps your listeners gain the most out of your testimony. Jesus often used parables and stories to relay His message to His listeners. Given that was not common in His day, the disciples asked Jesus, "Why do you tell stories?"

Jesus replied:

> *"…if there is no readiness, any trace of receptivity soon disappears. That's why I tell stories: to create readiness, to nudge people toward receptive insight"*
> (Matthew 13: 12-13 MSG).

Stories can enable listeners to be more receptive to new information or different perspectives. Stories that are relatable and have purpose draw us into the narrative, often causing us to want to know more. Rick Warren expands on why Jesus told stories in his blog *Communicating More Like Jesus*.[5] He shares, "Jesus told stories to make a point, to teach a spiritual truth." We also know that Jesus told stories in the context of relationship. He wanted people to be drawn to the truth.

Ultimately, the goal of sharing your faith story is to facilitate transformation in the lives of your listeners. An organized story increases the likelihood that your audience will be receptive, making it more likely for them to experience a personal connection.

If God has asked us to make the most of every opportunity to share our story of love, hope, and faith, then we need to be prepared to share it in a way that helps people be receptive, understand, and follow it. God nudges us to share our journey, not haphazardly, but with intention and purpose.

Three steps can help you maximize organizing your faith story so that listeners can gain the most from hearing it while also remaining flexible with telling it.

The three organizing steps are:

1. **Map Your Spiritual Journey**: Our stories often contain many events and rich details, but most people are not prepared to listen to all those details in one sitting. Taking time to reflect on your life's journey and determining the key milestones and events illuminating your faith journey will allow you to be more intentional with what you choose to share and with whom.

---

[5] Rick Warren Blog: *Communicating More Like Jesus: part 4.* June 3, 2022.

2. **Outline Your Story**: When you begin with an outline, creating and delivering a cohesive story is much easier. Before diving into the details, getting clear on your big-picture story elements is key to listener engagement and story flow.

3. **Bring Your Story to Life**: You'll want to share enough details to bring your story outline to life without distracting or confusing your listeners with too much information. Tapping into a few storytelling basics, along with adding pertinent details with purpose, enables you to deliver a cohesive story that keeps listeners engaged.

Organizing your story is not meant to limit you or confine you. Instead, it helps keep you focused and your listeners engaged so that the Holy Spirit can stir their souls as you speak.

Consider the impact of a well-organized story:

- It respects your audience's time, honoring their willingness to listen.

- It channels the essence of your experiences, distilling them into moments that resonate deeply with others.

- It becomes a channel through which the Holy Spirit can work, touching the hearts of your listeners.

Moreover, organizing your story is an act of obedience. When God calls you to share your experiences, He doesn't just ask for your words. He asks for your heart, your commitment, and your willingness to honor His message. By organizing your story, you are aligning yourself with God's purpose, embracing the responsibility of spreading His divine message of hope and faith.

So, as you enter the following chapters on organizing your story, remember that you're not just shaping words; you're creating a story of transformation. Through your story, you become a messenger of God's love, connecting hearts and illuminating a path to deeper faith.

Let's get started on mapping out your spiritual journey.

Chapter 4

Map Your Spiritual Journey

It's easier to get to your destination if you use a map. Or at least that's how it used to be before GPS! With GPS, we can drive on "autopilot." This works well when you're in a car, but if you leave your testimony story on autopilot, it could lead where you didn't intend to go. You could even get lost!

Mapping your faith journey helps you decide intentionally where you plan to go with your story. It helps you decide what part of your story to share and with whom. It gives you direction and provides alternative routes based on the listener's needs.

This mapping process is called a *Spiritual Autobiography*. It's simply a way to look at how God has worked in and throughout your life. It's charting the life events that have influenced who you are, and God's influence and impact on your life.

Taking time to map out your story will help you to be able to pull out what matters, to find the unique parts of your story, and to shape that into something meaningful in a way that points your listeners to Jesus. It also allows you to step back and reflect on your life to see where you can encourage others because of your unique journey.

Mapping your faith journey can help you achieve these goals:

- To quickly identify the stories you can share by reflecting on your life journey.
- To identify key events and turning points, enabling you to be intentional with what you focus your story around.
- To create a bank of short five-minute stories that can be shared independently or in combination.

Your life story is not one event, and God's grace does not show up only once in your life. Your story will be constantly updated as it unfolds. This allows you to share your story in many forms with whoever God puts on your life's path.

Through doing this mapping exercise for myself, I have recognized that I have a unique set of circumstances that only certain people will resonate with. These experiences have allowed Jesus to use my story to make Himself known to others.

For example, I came to know Jesus as my Savior in middle school. Still, as my life unfolded, I learned much more about God's grace, love, and character when I struggled as a single woman in my late thirties and early forties. Since then, God has put many women in my path who are experiencing those same struggles. I can then share the hope I found in Jesus during that season of my life and encourage them to seek Him. God has done the same for other seasons, such as being an older mom, and, more recently, my cancer journey.

Mapping Your Spiritual Autobiography

Mapping your faith journey is not a new concept. There are many ways to approach reflecting on and documenting your faith journey. Two approaches have worked well for my clients.

Approach 1: The Brain Dump

The first is to do a "brain dump" of everything that comes to mind that affected your faith journey: events, turning points, people, etc. Your goal is to write anything that comes to mind about your faith journey without stopping to assess the value of what you are writing. With prayer, God will illuminate what needs to come to mind for you.

With this approach, you can create a lot of information to draw from. It enables you to find the "jewels" or special parts that can be pulled out and emphasized within your story. It's also a resource to go back to as you look for ways to expand your bank of faith stories to tell.

Oscar used this approach to get something on paper for us to work with. He had sent me six pages of notes that still needed to be organized but allowed him to reflect on key milestones in his life. This was an easy way for him to start the process. Oscar said he initially wrote thirty pages, then brought it down to six for us to use.

Approach 2: Peaks and Valleys Timeline

Author Spencer Johnson, M.D., in his book *Peaks and Valleys: Making Good And Bad Times Work For You—At Work And In Life,* introduces the concept of looking at our life through the lens of "Peaks and Valleys."[6]

In this second approach, we expand on this concept by having you map your spiritual journey in addition to your work and/or life journey. You can do this by creating a visual timeline.

The idea is that everyone has a life story full of key events, issues, and influences.

---

[6] Author Spencer Johnson, M.D. in his book *Peaks and Valleys; Making Good And Bad Times Work For You – At Work And In Life.* Simone & Schuster, 2009.

Some were *positive*: "Peaks." Some were *negative*: "Valleys." Whether a peak or valley, some convinced you to follow Jesus, while others convinced you to trust Him more fully.

What determines whether something is a peak or a valley is entirely up to you. It's from your perspective and no one else's. Many people have a strong emotion connected with the event, which is either positive (joy, accomplishment) or negative (shame, grief). Identifying these emotions for yourself will also enable you to recognize that emotion in others, which can create a connection with your listener and provide an opportunity to share your story.

It's helpful to keep your focus fairly high-level for the first attempt at doing your map. You can go back and add more details later. The idea is not to get too mired down in the details but to create more of a "Big Picture" view of your turning points.

Let me demonstrate what that could look like using my own life story as an example. I have used short labels for each peak or valley to keep the visual simple. Adding a few more details to the label is fine. Just make sure not to write out every detail so that you don't lose sight of the key events and turning points.

Mary Ann's Spiritual Journey Example

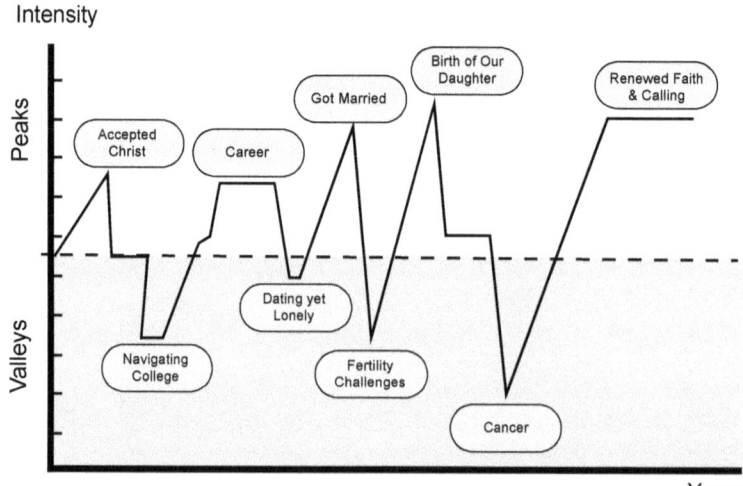

What if I don't have Peaks or Valleys?

You may wonder, what if all your experiences are above the line (viewed as positive), or what if all of them are below the line (viewed as negative)? If that is the perspective you feel your life journey represents, then I suggest you focus on the turning points, or milestone events, versus looking at it from the perspective of highs and lows. What is important to gain from the exercise is to identify how did those milestones or turning points impacted or changed your relationship with Jesus.

Question Prompts Help the Mapping Process

Ultimately, mapping your life's journey will help you identify the key aspects that can anchor your story and Jesus' role in your life. This helps you and your listener to get the most out of your story when you tell it.

Having a few prompts to reflect on helps get you started. Please don't feel the need to use them all. Some will resonate with you, and others may not.

- What were the key events, issues, and influences in your life?
- What emotion(s) did you feel as a result of the event? For example, did you feel fear, abandonment, shame or joy, happiness, fulfillment?
- Where have there been struggles, pain points, and sin that Jesus has specifically saved you from or helped you through?
- What were the circumstances through which you heard and responded to the gospel?
- What has Jesus done for you? Is there an answered prayer or miracle He provided?

- Have you experienced a failure? How did Jesus use it in your life?
- What is settled for you, and what are you still working through in your relationship with Jesus?

As you can imagine, completing your map could take some time. Set aside a quiet time to pray and reflect on your journey. It may be helpful to use the template timeline provided in the appendix of this book.

Mapping a Season in Your Life

Sometimes, the specific story you want to share with others is from a particular season in your life. Doing a Peaks and Valleys timeline can help you decide what to share about that season.

One of my clients, Ciara, lived through a difficult season of rebellion in her life by age 13. Ciara wanted to share her experiences with other teens and their parents to give them hope. Many people asked her and her family how they survived this difficult season, and Ciara felt ready to share it.

Ciara focused on doing a Peaks and Valleys timeline for just that season to help her start organizing the events and people in her story. It also helped her identify the moment she felt Jesus become real to her and some key turning points during her recovery process.

Mapping your whole life can be overwhelming. Choosing to start with a season in your life can help get the process going, along with identifying key events represented in a shorter window of time.

You may wish to use both approaches as part of your preparation. You could start with the brain dump approach and then go back and create a Peaks and Valleys timeline to visually pull out the turning points or key events you wish to spend more time developing into your testimony story.

> *"It is so easy for God's Story to get lost*
> *between the chapters of our own,*
> *so it is important to simplify and let*
> *his story be heard."*
>
> —Bob Shank, The Master's Program[7]

Is it Appropriate to Share the Hard Stuff?

I'm often asked, "Is it appropriate to share the hard stuff and/or the things that involve other people?" That is a difficult question to address with a blanket answer, and I am not an attorney or a trained therapist. Given that, I will share what I have observed and experienced for myself regarding this topic.

Part of being real and relevant with our faith story is sharing the difficult things that we've gone through and how Jesus met us there. These parts of our story can involve sensitive topics, family members, or others, and we need to be sensitive about sharing that.

Marcy Pusey, a certified trauma and resilience counselor, recommends that we must first process the event personally and come to a place of peace with it. Otherwise, it may be too overwhelming for us and our listeners if we are still processing the trauma as we share our story.[8]

---

[7] Bob Shank. Founder of Priority Living and The Master's Program. www.priori-tyliving.org.

[8] Pusey, Marcy. Overcoming Writer's Block: The Writer's Guide to Beating the Blank Page. Fresno, CA: Miramare Ponte Press, 2022.

If an event becomes part of your story that involves other people, then you need to ask their permission to share it or their name. In my own story, I share a very intimate discussion with my husband. It was critical to ask his permission before including it in my testimony.

Disclosing sensitive information might cause unexpected reactions from those involved. Be sensitive to how sharing your story may impact others (whether they are directly involved or not). An example of this for me was deciding to wait until our daughter was older before publicizing some of my testimony.

If you are questioning whether to include a sensitive part of your story, I suggest you seek the advice of a trained counselor, and if it involves other people, ask for their permission.

Five-Minute Stories Maximize Opportunities

Five-minute stories are short stories that can be delivered in five minutes or less. Identifying and creating a few five-minute faith stories is a valuable way to create more opportunities to share your testimony. These five-minute stories can be identified from your Peaks and Valleys timeline.

Creating a few five-minute faith stories enables you to address these listener needs:

- People have short attention spans; they appreciate a short story rather than a long one.
- These stories can represent different ways you experience Jesus in your life.
- It becomes easier to share a relevant story with different listeners who have different concerns or situations.
- It allows you to maximize your impact when timeframes are short.

- You can share these stories independently or in combination when more time is available.

For these reasons, I encourage you to create a bank of five-minute stories around different faith experiences that you have had on your life's journey. Identifying them ahead of time makes it easier to incorporate them into a faith conversation.

> *"One day, you will tell your story of how you overcame what you are going through now, and it will become part of someone else's survival guide."*[9]
>
> —Brian Solis, Author, Speaker, Futurist

Next, we'll focus on creating an outline for your story. When you begin with an outline, creating and delivering a cohesive story is much easier.

---

[9] Brian Solis. Author, speaker, futurist. Quote accessed from Instagram, August 16, 2020.

Chapter 5

Outline Your Story Elements

Outlining your story enables you to see the big picture and start to form the overall storyline without getting too mired down in the details. Adding structure makes your story easy to follow, but ultimately, the promptings of the Holy Spirit, your purpose, and your relationship with your audience should drive the delivery.

Given that, you'll want to learn how to add enough structure to your story so that it helps you enhance your relationship with your listeners and enables them to follow your story easily. For this reason, I suggest not trying to get to a specific "script," but to organize your story in a way that is easy for you to share yet stays on target with the points you want to get across. Creating an outline for your story helps you accomplish that.

Understanding the goals for each segment of a story structure outline can further help you maximize its function within your testimony and, ultimately, the delivery of your story.

The basic structure of a story—open, body, close (beginning, middle, end)—is familiar to us because we have all grown up hearing and sharing stories. Yet, most people enjoy a good story without thinking about what makes that story work.

A well-organized testimony story is a lot like a good book—you want to stay connected and interested. People of all ages love a good book and often retell parts of the book or recommend the book to others. Wouldn't it be great if your listeners did the same for your faith story?

Let's take a look at what authors do to make that happen. Let's pretend you need a book on a topic. You walk into a bookstore and pick a book off the shelf that interests you. You begin to read the introductory chapter... but then find it confusing, uninteresting, or that it did not meet your expectations. What would you do? Most people say they would stop reading and put the book back on the shelf.

Your listeners are no different when it comes to hearing the opening of your story. If your story does not capture their attention, feels aimless, or irrelevant, your listeners will check out mentally and/or physically.

A good book will start to draw you in from the beginning and quickly connect you to its main message or theme. This introduction gives the reader context to enter the story before the author adds other pertinent details.

Now, if you were to move into the rest of the book and see that there were no chapters—only endless text, page after page after page—would you be compelled to continue reading?

That would put off most people because we need breaks while reading. Breaking a book into chapters allows readers to absorb the content more easily, and the author to create building blocks that help us take in the entire story in a way that is compelling and manageable.

Within the chapters, the author brings the pertinent details to life by using examples, analogies, and vivid language to keep the reader engaged and interested.

Good books also feel seamless in connecting you from one chapter to another; this allows the reader to stay fully engaged with the storyline. It feels more purposeful versus random as you read through the book. Chapters also allow you, the reader, to reflect on what has just been read before moving on to what's next.

At the book's close, the author will have inspired you to take action or leave you pondering the topic with a new perspective. Your faith story should do the same for your listeners. You want them to desire to continue the conversation, take the next appropriate step, or leave with a new perspective on what faith in Jesus could look like for them.

With this book analogy in mind, let's look at how you can create an outline that supports sharing your story in a way that is cohesive and engaging.

Get Clear on Big-Picture Elements

When you allow the story structure outline to pull you out of the details, the big picture can emerge that will enable you to develop and deliver your story in a way audiences can receive. Getting clear on your big-picture story elements before diving into the details is key to engagement and story flow.

Listeners want the big picture for context; speakers need it to ensure that they are focused, intentional, and clear when delivering the details that bring it to life. The outline elements that are most helpful to you and your audience are:

- *Your story theme*: Deciding on a theme for your story can help to keep you focused as you pull your outline together. It is not necessarily stated to your listeners. The theme can be a main message and/or an aspect of God's character that you want to highlight for your listeners.

- *Opening*: The opening's purpose is to engage your listener(s) and provide a context for your story. People want context before details; they like to have a point of reference before taking on other pertinent information.

- *Body*: You want to create a logical unfolding of your story while making it manageable for your listeners to take in the information being shared. Outlining your two to three key story events into chapters will help keep your story manageable for you to share and for listeners to receive.

- *Closing*: The close should be purposeful. Use it to anchor your main message and extend an invitation to take the next appropriate step.

Each of these elements plays an important role in a well-told story. When you create and use an outline, it helps you, the speaker, stay focused, and helps the listener understand and follow your story, which leads to greater connection and engagement.

Outlining Made Simple

Outlining your story is an important step to focusing and managing your story details. Utilizing a template and a simple approach to create an outline helps you to be able to adapt to your listeners' needs and the Holy Spirit's guidance when it comes time to share your story.

I'd like to share how I outlined my testimony for a church women's event as an example. The purpose of the event was to have four church members each share their testimony as a way for us to get to know each other. We were asked to share for 20 minutes. There were about 100 women of all ages in attendance, members of our church and other guests.

In preparation, I took four simple steps to help me narrow down my life story for this event into a usable outline.

Step 1: *Reflect and Pray*

I returned to my Peaks and Valleys timeline and prayed, asking the Lord to help me narrow down 50-plus years of life experience into a few areas that *He* thought these women would resonate with. What He wanted me to focus on for these ladies that aligned with His purposes.

Step 2: *Select Events*

Based on my prayer time, I selected three events: two answered prayers (Peaks) and one miracle of mercy (Valley). Each represented a miracle from God and a deepening of my trust in Him.

Step 3: *Give it Focus*

I decided on these three events because they worked well together to represent the theme that I felt God wanted my audience to walk away with, which was: Our God is a God of miracles—give Him the desires of your heart, make Him Lord, and let Him perform a miracle in you.

Step 4: *Outline the Story Pieces*

Once I decided on the three events, I created an outline of them using a template I had created. I also added key descriptors within each section as prompts for myself to use when delivering it.

Outline Your Story Example: Mary Ann at Church Women's Event

Your Story Theme:

God of Miracles—Give God the desires of your heart, make Him Lord, and let Him perform a miracle in you.

Opening / transitioning into your story:

Have you ever thought about the statistics in your life and how they define you? Or how we let culture define us by those statistics?

Our God is not a God of statistics; He is a God of love and miracles! Let me share some of mine...

Body of your story: 1st Chapter

Stat: Perception of feeling like 1/million

Dallas; one man for every three ladies (all beautiful), hard to find a man over age 40 that still wants to get married and have children.

Scripture: Psalms 37:4 *"Delight yourself in the Lord and He will give you the desires of your heart."*

Jesus said to me: I want you to get two things straight:
* When dating use 5 C's Criteria: Christian, Compatible, Communication, Commitment, and Chemistry
* Become the woman that man will want to marry—see the hypocrisy in my own life.

First Miracle—Husband Donnie

Body: 2nd Chapter

Stat: 2% chance of getting pregnant at 44
- Fertility help or not?
- Foster Care / adoption route
- Pregnant God's way

Second Miracle—Daughter Jordan—Gave birth the next February at age 45

Transition: Nice if the story stopped there, but that would be short of *the real transformation* God did in me.

Body: 3rd Chapter

Stat: 45 Million people with Herpes
- I am one of them = Veil of guilt and shame
- Affected faith and relationships
- *"He does not treat us as our sins deserve or repay us according to our iniquities"* Psalm 103:10.
- Three conversations that changed Donnie's heart.

Third Miracle—God redefined my sin and identity through His grace and mercy.

Concluding Your Story:

If the statistics in your life aren't going as you desire, take them to the foot of the cross. Jesus wants to be the one who takes away our veil of shame, grief, and resistance so that we are not in bondage any longer. He is the way and the answer, and He will do that for each one of us if we just ask Him.

You can read the entire testimony I shared based on this outline in Chapter 15: *Steps of Courage*.

Ciara is another example of creating an outline. She and I used the template to organize the events from her Peaks and Valleys timeline map to create the following outline for her story.

Redeemed from Rebellion: Ciara's Story Outline

Your Story Theme:

There is hope, and God's love can redeem us no matter our age or circumstances.

Opening / transition into your story:

- Rebellion impacts everyone! Understanding rebellion is not easy because it's not a reaction to logic. It's ugly for those going through it and family members on the sidelines.
- Today I going to share my own personal journey through rebellion and how God's grace changed everything for me. My hope is that you will be encouraged that can redeem things in your life the way He has redeemed mine.

Body of your story: 1st Chapter:

Trigger events that led to rebellion

- Initial rebellion: my feelings of being out of control and rejected
- Rebellion often not a result of "intent" rather a result of feeling out-of-control
- What rebellion looked like at our house
- I wasn't living, I was surviving

Body: 2nd Chapter:

The process out of rebellion: It's not linear

- School & Butterflies; *"Two steps forward, one step backward!"*
- I learned to stay in the process; key to changing the trajectory of my life
- 5 lessons:
    - o Be vulnerable
    - o Take responsibility
    - o Know it is a process
    - o Accept help
    - o Family love & support make a difference

Body: 3rd Chapter:

Redemption: God's Grace

- When/how I decided to surrender to God—how God met me & transformed my heart
- The final piece of the puzzle: Wild Horses camp
- My journey now

Concluding Your Story:

Hope for the future & aspirations

Jesus saved me and He's given me the opportunity to bring hope and peace to others through my testimony.

The fact that I can even say that is truly a miracle. Remember, this is coming from a kid who was a bully, a liar, and a thief.
- This isn't just a redemption story, it is an empowerment story.
- But actually, it was only just the beginning of my bright future. I am daily growing my relationship with Jesus. My life is extra-ordinarily better. And I am excited for what the future holds. I have the best family that supports me the whole way. I have a life worth fighting for.
- Your future is worth fighting for just like mine was. He saved us all for a reason!
- What has He saved you from? How will you use that to help others?

Just like I believe God is using my story to impart hope, I want to challenge you to ask yourself:

What are you going to allow God to do with your story?

Once Ciara completed this outline, she felt much better about adding the pertinent details to the story and letting go of things that were not as important to include. As expected, it took several revisions over a few months to get to the place where Ciara liked her story and was ready to practice it. Her full testimony based on this outline can be found in Chapter 13: *Encouraging the Next Generation.*

The Gift of Outlining Your Story

We all have many stories of God's grace in our lives. By mapping and outlining your spiritual journey events, you are positioning your stories for God to use with those in your circle of influence and beyond.

For example, because I had done the work to identify and outline the three events in my story, I have now been able to share each one separately as a shorter testimony with individuals that God has put in my circle of influence. I have shared my "wishing for a husband" and/or "desire for a child" with many women and family members who struggle with God's timing in getting married or starting a family.

Outlining your stories provides a useful tool for practicing and reference notes, if needed, when you share your story. Keeping your outline high-level also gives you greater flexibility when using it as a tool to share your story in various settings.

The key is to keep it simple, high-level, and allow the Holy Spirit to guide you as you move forward to add in the pertinent details.

To add your pertinent details with purpose, one more thing you'll want to consider is who will be listening. In the next chapter, you will learn what to consider when sharing with an individual versus sharing in a group setting.

Chapter 6
Consider Who Will Be Listening

A relevant story is compelling! To be able to provide your listeners with a relevant story, you want to take into consideration their personality, concerns, interests, and spiritual awareness. Consider what they may want and need to know to take a personal step in their own faith journey.

This could impact the sequence of your story, what you choose to emphasize, or whether you will be focusing on one specific faith story or linking a few five-minute stories together. You also want to consider if you will be sharing your story with an individual, small group, or a larger group. Each of these has implications for how you enter your story, along with how you unfold the story and invite them into the next step.

Sharing With An Individual

We often share our faith story with only one person. That person may be a neighbor, co-worker, friend, or family member who has just shared a concern or challenge they are facing. Because you care about them, you'll want to share a part of your journey that can be an encouragement to them.

You may have been through a similar experience that enables you to identify with the emotion or situation they are experiencing.

This creates an opportunity to share your faith testimony in the context of your relationship with them.

If your listener is a non-believer, you have an opportunity to share your relationship with Jesus and to help your listener connect with His love and grace for them. When sharing with a non-believer, taking the extra step to ensure you include the gospel message can help them understand the relevance of the gospel when shared in the context of your story.

There may also be times when the purpose of sharing your faith story is to give a believer renewed hope and faith in times of trials or discouragement. As the body of Christ, we want to be of encouragement and strengthen the faith of our brothers and sisters.

When sharing with an individual, you are in a conversation with them. Because it is a two-way dialog, your story should be a natural extension of the conversation. Based on something they said that concerns them in their own life, you could then transition into your faith story. It could be as simple as "I hear you saying you are feeling (lonely, anxious, regretful). I have felt that way, too. Can I tell you more about my experience with that?"

Recently, I've had a few conversations like these around poor choices and shame. A family member shared how they'd made a poor choice and was struggling with the consequences and continued guilt of that choice. I asked permission to share a time I'd made a poor choice in my own life and how God helped me through it. From there, I shared my testimony, remaining flexible to keep it conversational.

I believe asking permission to share your story is important in these cases. Sharing our testimony in a one-to-one setting should be in response to where the other person is coming from, not an evangelistic tool to be thrust upon an unsuspecting soul—especially if they are personally grappling with the consequences of sin themselves.

Sarah Young, the author of *Jesus Calling*, states, "We are on holy ground in those situations and need to be relying on the Holy Spirit to guide us in discernment to share our story."[10] We are reminded in 1 Peter 3: 15 (NIV) that God encourages us to share our hope "with gentleness and respect."

The key to staying present with your listener is taking the time *in advance* to prepare and know your story's faith implications. This allows you to share your story in a concise, intentional way that points them to Jesus.

Taking time to map and prepare your faith stories in advance allows you to be ready in the moment to meet the needs of your listener while staying flexible in the conversation. It's then easier to stop and answer questions, clarify a confused look, or determine whether the conversation should continue or be picked up later. It also frees you up to be a better listener when you have asked them a question or they express a concern.

Speaking to a Small Group

For our purposes, a small group is defined as three to fifteen people. You may be having coffee with a few friends or with your small group Bible study or at a luncheon with a group, etc.

Often in these settings you know some, if not all, the people listening. The opportunity to share your testimony may have been

---

[10] Sarah Young. *Jesus Calling*, published by Thomas Nelson 2008. Reference from October 31 devotional page.

sparked by something said in the conversation or your group may have asked you to share your story to get to know you.

Although you want to be conversational in these settings, you still want to have your story organized, and to have considered what would be relevant to emphasize for this group within your story.

Consider if there has been a concern, interest, or topic that has been on the minds of the group or a recent event that has implications for the group. As you share your story, you are then able to be intentional in asking questions and using inclusive language that helps your story become relevant. You can then also share how we are all part of God's bigger story.

Speaking To A Larger Group

When speaking to a larger group it becomes more formal. I'm not suggesting you change from a conversational style to a formal presentation style. Still, there are considerations that are unique to a larger group setting that you can address to ensure that your story or message is heard in a clear, relevant, and purposeful way.

One primary difference is that, typically, you do not know everyone in the audience. However, you still want to consider what they care about individually and collectively so that you can choose relatable parts of your journey to include in your story or message.

For example, Ciara was given the opportunity to share her redeemed from rebellion story at a youth group meeting with fifty teens and parents attending. I asked her what she thought this group would want to know. Ciara thought of three things:

- Is this normal?
- Is there hope?
- What can I do?

People had already been asking her and her family these types of questions. Our goal was to ensure that those three questions were addressed within her story.

If given some forethought, you, too, can discern what your audience might be interested in, concerned about, or connect with. For Christian speakers, the audiences can vary a lot. The group may consist of parents, church members, non-believers and believers, businesspeople, and youth groups—the list is endless. Yet, even with a varied audience, you can deliver a story that has meaning and impact for them.

In The Message Bible, we are reminded that Jesus modeled sharing stories in a way that fit His listeners' experiences.

> *"With many stories like these, He presented*
> *His message to them, fitting the stories to their*
> *experience and maturity. He was never without*
> *a story when He spoke"* (Mark 4:33, MSG).

The idea here is that if you are asked to share with a larger group, take a few minutes to consider them as individuals (or sub-groups) to discern what they are interested in or care about so that you can personalize your story to be relevant to them. I will also share more about engagement tools for personalizing your story in Part 4: *Value Your Audience.*

Story Timeframes: Three Minutes Can Change a life!

Today, more than ever, our culture is used to taking in information and stories in less time. We have all been conditioned by social media to assess quickly whether we want to stay engaged with a story or move on.

Research conducted by Microsoft backs this up.[11] They found that the average attention span of Gen Z individuals was only about eight seconds, four seconds less than that of Millennials. Given that, you'll want to be aware of the amount of time you take to share your story and use that time well to make your point while maintaining engagement.

To maximize the opportunities to share your story in various settings, consider adapting your story for a few different timeframes. A good place to start is with a solid five-minute version and then scale it back to three minutes so you can more easily share it in a conversation.

Sam Horn, author of *Got Your Attention,* shares that we should not underestimate the power of a three-minute talk. Regardless of the time we are given, every occasion can become an opportunity to make a significant impact. She states:

> *"You can change a life in three minutes. You can say something that will inspire someone in the audience to launch a business, write a book, contribute to a worthy cause, be a better parent or leader. You can say something people haven't heard before that opens people's eyes and facilitates a life-changing epiphany."*[12]

Your three-minute testimony has the power to do that. Whether short or long, your faith story can impact your listeners' lives. The Holy Spirit will be working through you to make that difference.

---

[11] The study led by Microsoft Canada on how technology has affected attention spans, conducted 2015. Sourced through Google on April 30, 2024.

[12] Sam Horn. *Got Your Attention: How to Create Intrigue and Connect with Anyone,* 2015. LinkedIn article "Why Every Speaking Opportunity Matters" accessed September 20, 2017.

Consider also creating a longer version of your story by linking together two to three shorter five-minute faith stories from your spiritual journey map to create a 15- to 20-minute version that would be appropriate in a group setting. The ideas and tools in this book can be used for all these various timeframes.

Being able to deliver a relevant story that touches the hearts and minds of your listeners has the ability to connect your listeners to God's love and transformation for them personally. How rewarding is that?

Now that you have considered who will be listening, let's move on to how to add your pertinent details in a way that keeps them engaged throughout your story.

Example: Our Family Reunion

This example represents how God works through us when we pursue preparing our messages and stories with a compassionate concern for our listeners and seek His guidance.

Context: Jim's family is about to hold their first family reunion and he has been asked to share a message on Sunday morning. Jim's desire is to share a message that would touch everybody's heart. He wants to share a story of faith that would encourage them and glorify God.

Jim describes his extended family: we're not a tightly knit family. Everyone is coming from different places; their life experiences and their perspectives are different. And I am not sure where they stand with their individual faiths.

In preparation, Jim spent time in prayer to ask God what He wanted shared with Jim's family.

Here is a recap of what Jim felt guided to share that Sunday. He entered his story with an attitude of humility and transparency.

Our Family Reunion

I want to share my personal process and journey to share this message with you today.

I initially researched the Bible for stories about families and reunions, such as:

- Joseph and his brothers selling him into slavery and how it shows that God can use all things for good for those who love him.

- The Prodigal Son represents a wonderful story of a father's love and family reunion, even after bad behavior and poor choices.

- The Wedding of Cain, where Jesus did his first public miracle amid a family wedding celebration.

I thought to myself, *Maybe that's what everybody needs to hear and understand about God's grace and bringing family members together.* But then I thought, *No, that's not the story.*

I want you to know I talked to a lot of people to prepare myself for today. I kept thinking, what would be the best use of this time we have together?

One person shared with me that I should spend time listening to God first to seek His guidance for you. That really resonated with me, so I have spent some quiet time in prayer and listening for God to guide me in what I should share with you this morning. (Everyone was now leaning in to hear my next words.)

God told me to tell you, "*I love you... I love you.*" (I looked at each person and made eye contact.) Then God said to tell you, "*I see you... I see you.*"

My sister had previously shared a story of an incident that happened on the way to the reunion, where she felt God was not watching out for her. This message touched her deeply, personally, and spiritually.

After that, I said, "God asked me to share two more things with each of you. God told me to tell you, each and every one of you, '*I chose you... I chose you.*' Then one of the most important things He wants me to tell you is, '*I'm coming back for you... I am coming back for you.*'"

I then went on to tie it all together by bringing it back to family reunions. This family reunion is temporary, but the ultimate and final reunion to come will be when Jesus returns to gather up His chosen. This then led to a discussion about comparing the invitation to come to this family meeting to the invitation that God has given us to join his family.

Outcome: Jim said he felt God's presence and that several family members began to share stories that related to his message.

He felt he was able to go beyond just sharing information (his traditional academic style) to giving his family a message that communicated the transformative power that was available to them personally through Jesus Christ.

Jim was also able to have several follow-up conversations and one-on-one prayers with family members, one of whom was his grandnephew (age 13), who shared that he had always wondered if God even knew who he was. He said he now understood that God loves him, sees him, and chose him to be in His family.

His story is an example of how taking time to consider the needs of your listeners and seek God's guidance produces a relevant and impactful message—a story that blesses people and honors God.

Chapter 7
Bring Your Story to Life

Prayer Coach Lisa Newmeyer shares a good analogy for the role that structure plays in an effective story. She says, "A story without structure is like our bodies would be without our bones. We would not be able to function properly. But if you focus only on your body, you really aren't living life."

She is saying that our bones are the internal, unseen part of the body that allows us to function and move properly. But that structure is only one part of what makes us feel fully alive and functioning. It's when we can channel the essence of our experiences and distill them into moments that resonate deeply with others that it gives our story life. Ultimately, it is our relationship with God as revealed through our story that facilitates transformation for our listeners.

This is why I advocate for the idea that the structure of your story should never trump your relationships with God and your listeners. If your story is structured to the point where you have no flexibility, then you will likely not allow yourself to go "off script" when the Holy Spirit prompts you.

Yet, there is still value in providing enough structure to give your story a strong foundation and then adding the pertinent details that can bring your story to life for your listeners. The key to adding your pertinent details with purpose is to keep in mind who will be listening. From there, you can take your story outline and bring it to life with them in mind.

As we explore this further, remember that you're not just shaping words; you're creating a story of transformation. How you choose to open, unfold the body, and close your story helps to create a memorable and transformative experience for listeners.

Build on a Strong Foundation

In the next few chapters, you will be building on the work you've already done to create your outline. Now, we'll focus on how to incorporate your story details with a purpose of expanding on that outline.

To recap the story basics, they include:

- *Opening*: The opening's purpose is to engage your listeners and provide a context for the story. People want context before details. They need and want a point of reference before taking on other pertinent information.

- *Body*: The body logically unfolds your story while making it manageable for your listeners to take in the information being shared.

- *Closing*: The close anchors your main message and/or extends an invitation to take the next appropriate step.

The next three chapters are dedicated to adding depth and examples for the opening, body and closing of your story. At this point, I want to share more about the concept of identifying and having a story theme to help you illuminate God's character within your story.

Create Focus with a Story Theme

Given that most people cannot take in your whole life story or the magnitude of God in one sitting, it is helpful to determine a theme for your story that can illuminate an aspect of God's character. This will help you determine what part(s) of your story to share while adding your details with purpose.

You'll want to be intentional with where you take the storyline. Identifying your story theme provides a way to keep you focused and leads to a more concise story. One way to establish your story theme is to ask yourself:

What do I want my audience to think about or focus on most about God?

Some examples of themes prior clients have focused their stories on are:

- Release your grip and let God's better plan for you unfold.
- Seek the truth of who God says you are... not what the world says you are.
- With God, you are capable of more than you know.
- God doesn't need our expertise; He needs our obedience.
- Every one of us is called to be heroic for the Kingdom.
- There is hope, and God's love can redeem us no matter our age or circumstances.

As you can see, it doesn't need to be long or complicated. Keep it simple and allow it to focus and guide your story.

When you are preparing to share with a group, having a theme that anchors your story enables you to stay focused and provides your listeners with a clear message that gives them a new perspective, something to reflect on, or to take action on, whether you end up stating this theme with your listeners or not.

Illuminate God's Character

As Christians, the moral to our story—our theme— embodies that Jesus is the answer, that He is relevant to our lives, and can/will make a difference for us and them. Your story is often the vehicle that the Holy Spirit uses to make that evident to listeners.

Yet, it can also be hard for us to describe Him in His fullness. Given that, consider focusing on, or highlighting, one or two characteristics of God.

For example, His provision, His mercy, His strength, and His grace... This can make it easier for non-believers to relate to Him and what He desires for us and them. Ultimately, it is God's character that reveals Jesus as our Savior.

Pray and ask God to guide you in this. Some prayer questions you may ask Him:

- Father, what aspect of Your character do You want my listener to learn about?
- Father, how does that relate to my listener?
- Father, how do You want me to express that through my story?

Trust that He will guide you to what is relevant for your listeners at this time.

Identifying your story theme and the character of God you want to focus on gives you direction before moving forward with adding the details of your story. It will also help you pull out the unique parts of your story and shape them into something meaningful for your listeners.

Now it's time to expand on your outline using your story theme to create a story that will engage your listeners and create Kingdom ripples.

Chapter 8
Openings That Engage

The purpose of an opening is to pique interest and start to provide context for your story. You are essentially helping transition your listener's mind from whatever they were thinking about to your story's theme so that they can take in the rest of your story in a meaningful way. Listeners prefer to have context before hearing all the details.

To achieve that, a good opening will facilitate the following:

- Engages your listeners from the start with something interesting that also sets up the focus of your story with purpose.
- Begins to position your story theme and the character of God you want your listeners to think about or act upon moving forward.
- Sets the tone, reflecting your heart and personal style with your listeners.

The opening is the one part of your story that can be very different between sharing with an individual and sharing with a group.

When opening with an individual, you enter your story based on your listener and how the conversation has gone up to the point of deciding to share your story. Given this, the transition into your story will often come naturally. Where they have shared a concern or situation, it provides an opportunity for you to share your story to encourage greater hope and faith for them.

With an individual, it often comes in the form of asking a question or making a statement based on what is already happening in the conversation, providing a door to sharing your story.

For example, when a friend is struggling with God's timing for marriage, I could say something like, "Sounds like you wish God would provide a spouse for you sooner. Can I share what He showed me as I struggled with being single for so long?"

You'll want to keep it simple and authentic as you enter into your story when speaking with individuals. Ask the Holy Spirit to guide you in taking an approach that will meet their needs.

When you are planning to share in a group setting, there is understandably more formality to the way you open. Given that a group is composed of a variety of people with various backgrounds, there is a greater need to provide a point of entry to your story that sets both the context and engages their attention before you dive into the details. Otherwise, they may feel lost or confused about where you are going with your story or its purpose.

There are various options to engage your listeners and pique their interest, along with helping to set a proper context. How you choose to open will largely depend on your personal style, setting, and the amount of time you have.

In the following pages, I share examples of ways my clients have engaged their listeners. These examples are not in order of preference, nor is one better than another. My hope is that these will spark some ideas for you and your story's opening.

These examples represent a variety of people and situations, and although many are used in a group setting, there is value in considering using them when sharing with an individual.

The key is to keep your listeners and your style in mind so that it feels natural to you and a good fit to begin your story with.

Here are a few of the more common techniques for opening your story:

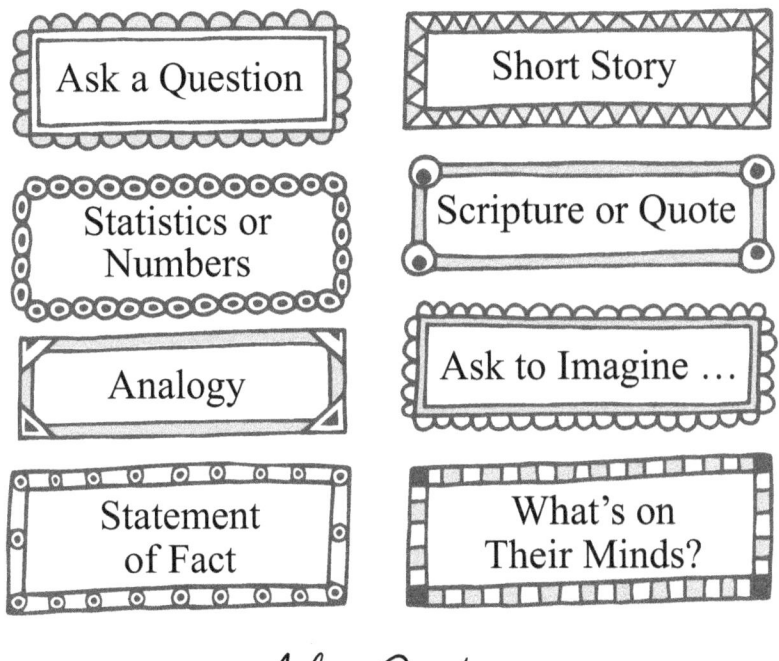

Ask a Question | Short Story

Statistics or Numbers | Scripture or Quote

Analogy | Ask to Imagine ...

Statement of Fact | What's on Their Minds?

Ask a Question

Questions get us thinking. Asking a question (rhetorical or otherwise) is a great way to involve and engage the audience. You may choose to ask one question or a few. The key is to be intentional so that the question and its answer are relevant to your story and listeners. Once you have asked the question, *pause* for a moment to let it sink in. People need time to process your question in their minds for it to be effective.

Example: Becca's opening questions for the college graduation speech:

> Ladies and gentlemen, it is an honor to represent our graduating class today. Let me begin by asking you a question.
>
> If you were in a position to give a scholarship to a young student, what qualities would you be looking for and willing to invest in?
>
> Now, what would happen if you learned this person of interest was... a drug addict... a perpetual liar, and... living in an all-girl lockdown residential treatment center?
>
> Would you still want to invest in that person?
>
> That person was me, and a few short years ago, our university administration did just that—they took a risk, saw past my life's adversity, and extended a scholarship that helped me to turn my life around and begin to learn what I am truly capable of. Like many graduates today, I came to the university with a background that affected how I approached school and life.

Example: Testimony in group setting:

> Have you ever done something in your past that you hold against yourself? A mistake or bad choice where you felt you could not be forgiven?
>
> I have. Today, I want to share that experience with you and how God helped me through it.

Example: Student to a panel of teachers/parents:

When you think of the astronaut Neil Armstrong, film producer Steven Spielberg, and J.W. Marriott, the founder of the Marriott hotel chain, would you be inclined to add my name to that list?

Well, you can! Because we have all earned Eagle Scout. Today, I want to show you the effort it took to earn Eagle Scout and how God helped me through the process.

When we pose a question to the audience, the story has a greater opportunity to feel like *our* story, not just your story. The audience feels they are participating in, or affected by, a journey that has implications for them.

Statistics / Numbers

Statistics or numbers can quickly paint a picture of the situation to help set the context. The key to using statistics/numbers is to use only a few. If you stick to three or fewer, they carry a lot more power to influence than a long list of numbers shared all at once.

Example: You may recall from Chapter 1 that Oscar used numbers to gain the attention of his audience quickly and then linked those numbers to the purpose of his talk. He was able to reduce years of life experiences down to three numbers that summarized his gang lifestyle.

"I would like to share some significant numbers with you: 20, 15, and 2.

20 (the number of years I have spent in prison)

15 (the number of felonies counted against me)

2 (times stabbed; one in prison and one on the streets)"

Example: Ambassador Hall when speaking about World Hunger:

- 2,500 scripture verses deal with the poor—the most talked about theme in the Bible.

- Half the people in the world live on less than $2 a day.

Example: Ministry leader as to why they focus on the next generation:

- According to Youth Policy, 60% of the people in the Middle East are currently under the age of 25.

Analogy

Contrasting something familiar to your audience with something new or not normally considered from that perspective can quickly connect the information in an understandable way.

Example: Nonprofit ministry leader presenting to a group of businesspeople:

> Uber, Apple, and Airbnb: Each one of these businesses changed the paradigm of their industry. Today, I want to talk to you about how The Cause Ministry is changing the paradigm for nonprofits and their ability to be sustainable.

Example: Individual to a small group:

Matt was asked to share his testimony with a couples' group. He had normally only shared his testimony with men, but now he was asked to share it in a mixed setting. He wanted to help the entire group relate to his challenge. He chose to combine a question with an analogy.

> I want to start by asking you a question. Have you ever been in a situation where you were

trying to accomplish something and got in over your head? Maybe you had the best intentions, yet you find yourself unable to pull it off.

Maybe in your life, that is a diet. You have a 30-day plan; you want to stay on the diet... and then two days into it, you find yourself eating all the chocolate cake in the refrigerator.

Or maybe it's a New Year's resolution, and you have a workout plan... and a couple of days into it, you are lying on the couch.

Can anybody identify with these kinds of resolutions and plans?

Well, I found myself in a situation a bit more drastic than that. In a situation with the best of intentions, with a plan in place, and yet, I could not overcome my issue in my own strength. My issue?... I was addicted to pornography.

Matt shared how a specific program called F.U.E.L. and his relationship with Jesus helped him regain his life and conquer his addiction.

Statement of Fact

A simple statement or known fact can quickly pique interest and get you started on your story's theme with focus.

Example: Ciara sharing with other youth and their family members:

"Rebellion impacts everyone! Understanding rebellion is not easy because it's not a reaction to logic. It's ugly for those going through it and for the family members on the sidelines."

Example: Non-profit ministry that uses soccer to reach kids for Christ:

> Did you know that more people watched the World Cup this year than the first 20 Super Bowls combined?

> Soccer is universal! Because it is a world sport, it enables us to reach people we are normally unable to reach with the gospel. That is where our ministry comes in... Our mission is to…

Short Story

A short story can quickly bring the audience into the bigger story when tied to the theme or message you want the audience to focus on. When you choose to share a story about Jesus from the Bible, you are bringing your listeners into God's bigger story. Sharing a story about Jesus is one of the most influential ways to connect your story to the transforming power that Jesus has for all of us.

Example: Ministry spokesperson to church missions board:

> I would like to begin by sharing a story about James. He is an established businessman who is active in the community and leads a 'country club' life. He joined us a few years ago on a trip to Malawi to see firsthand what life in Africa is like. On that trip, God grabbed his heart and began to open his eyes to the possibilities of the difference he could make to the quality of life of many children and families in Malawi. He also decided to donate the country club dues to projects that affect Malawi—through that God transformed him and impacted others.

His story theme: By getting involved with what God is doing in Africa, you too can be transformed as individuals and as a church.

Example: Richard with his men's group.

> I remember our trip to Israel in 2008—we sailed out of Tiberius on the Sea of Galilee early one morning. Suddenly, our boat got caught in a storm! In the early morning! Deck chairs were sliding to the rails, and one had a woman sitting in it. Deckhands saved her! It became another one of those spiritual markers Jesus put into my life. You know, those sometimes little but significant events that come into your life where you realize, 'I think God just talked to me.'
>
> Jesus asks us to go, and He puts conflict in our lives—but He is with us to overcome our fears and, through faith, give us hope for ourselves and others.
>
> *"As evening came, Jesus said to his disciples, 'Let's cross to the other side of the lake.' So, they took Jesus in the boat and started out, leaving the crowds behind (although other boats followed). But soon a fierce storm came up. High waves were breaking into the boat, and it began to fill with water. Jesus was sleeping at the back of the boat with his head on a cushion. The disciples woke Him up, shouting, 'Teacher, don't you care that we're going to drown?' When Jesus woke up, He rebuked the wind and said to the waves, 'Silence! Be still!' Suddenly, the wind stopped, and there was a great calm. Then He asked them, 'Why are you afraid? Do you still have no faith?'"* (Mark 4:35-40, NLT).

Example: Ministry spokesperson sharing a Jesus story with a Christian business group:

> We are all created for a higher purpose and a deeper calling of God. Life will never make sense; life will never be meaningful for us until we find out what we are created to do. What does God intend to do with our life here on earth?

> I discovered this higher calling and a deeper purpose when I started reading the Bible. Luke 5 talks about the beautiful story where Peter, an experienced fisherman and businessman, went to Lake Tiberius, Galilee. But that night, he wasn't successful. He fished all night but caught nothing until Jesus Christ showed up and stepped into one of his boats, and He instructed him to do something very unique and very special.

> He said, "Peter, go into the deep water and lay down your nets." Their nets began to break. Their boat began to sink, to the point that Peter and his friends had to call their partners on the other boat to come and help them.

> Now I am standing here tonight, and I look at this beautiful room full of great leaders, men and women of God, and I don't know where your deep water is, but my deep water is in the Middle East.

> Your deep water might be scary, somewhere dark, somewhere that you feel uncomfortable going. But unless we are willing to obey the Lord Jesus Christ, leave everything behind, and

go to the deep water, we will never experience a net-breaking business, ministry, or family to the point that when Peter obeyed, a miracle took place, because He's the Lord of working miracles in our lives.

Well, let me tell you here tonight that our nets are breaking!

He went on to share how this group can be the partners that help them move forward with this miracle that God has provided for them. He also came back to this story throughout his presentation to connect his listeners to the meaning of following Jesus into deep waters and how that impacts them individually.

Scripture or Quotes

Scriptures and quotes can give context or provide a new perspective to a theme or direction you are taking with your story.

Example Scripture: Often used to highlight God's timing:

> *"And who knows but that you have come to your royal position for such a time as this?"*
> Esther 4:14b, NIV

Example Quote: To illuminate an idea or theme:

> "One day, you will tell your story of how you overcame what you are going through now, and it will become part of someone else's survival guide."
> Brian Solis, author, speaker, futurist

Ask the Audience to Imagine... or Put Themselves in Someone's Shoes

Asking the audience to imagine or picture something can be a very powerful way to put the audience in the shoes of the person or situation you are talking about.

Example: Non-profit ministry to potential supporters:

> Susan has a difficult decision to make. She is one of 20,000 San Diego women who are faced with deciding whether to keep a pregnancy each year. Susan's parents did not want her to stay in their home if she decided to keep the baby, and her boyfriend abandoned her when he found out. She felt she could no longer stay in school if she decided to have the baby.
>
> As you can imagine, all these factors weighed heavily on her mind—this decision was not easy! Yet, in the end, she decided to keep the baby, which meant she needed a place to live.
>
> She is one of our own. Her unborn child is also one of our own, which is why we created the 29: Eleven Maternity Home.
>
> As Christians, family, and a community, we feel called by God to make a difference for women like Susan. Our mission is to "Save a life and transform another." We desire to be part of the solution. We believe the Lord has plans for these ladies, their children, and for all of us.

Start with What is on Their Mind

There are times when a significant event has happened in the world, or your community, that presents an opportunity to speak to what is on your listeners' minds. Starting with addressing that event, concern, or opportunity demonstrates you are aware of it and care about how your listeners may be affected by it. As you transition into your story, this could provide yet another way to personalize for your audience.

Example: Individual

> I think we can all agree that COVID changed our world and our lives forever. We have each been affected by its impact. I would like to share how it impacted me during my cancer treatment and how, when I felt most alone, God used it to make His presence known to me at a deeper level.

As you can see, there are a variety of options to choose from that can pique your audience's attention and engage them into your story theme. Keep in mind that how you choose to engage your audience will be influenced by who is listening, your personal style, and your story's theme.

Once you have engaged your listeners' attention, you want to unfold your story in a way that maintains that engagement.

Chapter 9

Keep Engagement, Create Connections

Now that you have gained your listeners' attention with your opening, you want to keep them engaged and continue to create connections that build momentum.

The middle or body of your story contains the bulk of your story's details. The focus of this section is to create a logical unfolding of your story while making it manageable for your listeners to take in the information and remain engaged.

The goal is to manage those details so that your story has continuity and purpose. Applying these elements within the body of your story helps you to achieve that goal:

- *Create chapters*: People want and need breaks for the content to feel manageable to process. Creating chapters within your story helps to break the information into manageable pieces for listeners. You have already done most of the work to create chapters with your story outline. We'll build on that.

- *Add details with purpose*: The goal here is to share enough details to bring the story to life without distracting or confusing your listeners with too much information.

- *Create connections*: You create connections by linking your different chapters together so that your story has continuity, along with continuing to keep engagement and build momentum through examples, analogies, and lessons learned.

Create a Cohesive Story

Finding the storyline in all your details is more easily achieved when you apply the concept of creating chapters within your story. An analogy to this is acting in a play. Typically, there are three acts in a play, and we look forward to each act as it builds out the play's story. Similarly, your faith story could build on two to three events or turning points within your story. That helps to keep your listeners engaged, leading them to want to know the ending of your story.

I believe the idea of creating chapters within your story is one of the most underutilized structure tools, yet it provides tremendous value to you and your listeners. It is a simple way to add enough structure to make it easy for listeners to follow along, while also building momentum and engagement.

Once identified, each chapter helps you share an aspect of the overall story you wish to convey to your listeners. Start by determining which two to three chapters will help you harness your details meaningfully.

There are various ways to create and organize your story chapters. Here are a few ideas to get you thinking, beginning with the traditional testimony structure.

- Before, During, After
  - My life before Jesus
  - Circumstances for choosing to accept Jesus as my Lord and Savior
  - My transformed life today

When considering using this traditional approach to organizing your story chapters, keep in mind that this can also apply to other life situations—other than the point in time when you made a decision to follow Christ. It can also apply to different situations in your life where you share what was going on in your life before you turned that specific situation over to Jesus, then what unfolded as you trusted Him in that situation, and what has now transformed in you as a result.

- Chronological order: one client used decades to demonstrate how her perception of God's presence changed over time.
  - In my 20s...
  - In my 30s...
  - In my 40s...
- Sequencing events/turning points. (these often come from your spiritual journey map)
- Sequencing example from Ciara's story:
  - Trigger events that led to my rebellion
  - The process out of rebellion; it's not linear
  - Redemption: God's grace and my hope for the future
- Sequencing example from Oscar's story:
  - Childhood: unchosen circumstances
  - The Neighbor "hood": influences, choices, and consequences
  - My Homeboy Pastor Friend: Jesus was chasing after me
  - The God of 2nd Chances and a Life of Purpose

As you can see, there are various options for creating your story chapters. When you take the time to identify your story chapters, it also prepares you to make adjustments at the moment when your timeframe changes. It can help you to keep the integrity of your storyline while enabling you to release less important details when time is shortened or add more details if more time is made available.

You do not need to share these chapter titles with your listeners. Their main function is to help you organize your information in a meaningful way that is easy for listeners to receive.

Using this chapter approach helps you to know what details to keep versus what details to let go of because they do not support your chapter's message or theme. Using this chapter approach gives you a structured framework for filling in the pertinent details.

Add Details with Purpose

The goal here is to share enough details to bring your story to life without distracting, confusing, or boring your listeners with too much information. Sometimes it can be hard to determine what is pertinent versus what is distracting. There is no set formula for how to accomplish this. I found that allowing the Holy Spirit to guide you is best. Ultimately, you decide what stays and what to let go of.

To provide an example of removing details from a draft in order to produce something more concise, let's look at Oscar's "before" and "after" for the first chapter of his story. You will notice we took things out that didn't enhance the story or were not as relevant to his audience at this time. Depending on who Oscar is talking to, he could always put these parts back in if he wanted. For this specific event, he needed a 20-minute version of his story to share at a local high school.

Example: Oscar's "Before version" for Chapter 1 of his story: Highlights represent what we chose to take out.

> My name is Oscar. I was born in 1979, and that same year, a cardinal was assassinated in South America. His name was Oscar Romero, so my mom decided to name me after him. I look back and see how weird that sounds. I was from a middle-class family; there were seven of us, money was always tight, and my dad was an abusive, angry alcoholic. He would beat me every chance he got and call me a worthless piece of crap ever since I can remember. I honestly thought he hated me. I had my first sip of beer when I was six years old. I thought that it made me a grown-up. That was around the same time I was getting molested by the neighbor who happened to be my brother's best friend. I was scared to tell anybody, especially my parents, because I knew they would disown me.
>
> So, I promised myself that I would never let anyone make me feel powerless and vulnerable again. I was raised very Catholic, so I believed that everything that happened to me was God punishing me because I somehow deserved it. I started hating myself. I wished I could have been born to somebody else so my parents could love me. I started avoiding my parents, only coming out to eat when no one was around, or only eating at school. When my dad got angry, it would literally be a two- or three-day event. I would dread coming home because it would only be a matter of time before he would find a

reason to get angry at me. I hated being at home because it felt like I was constantly walking on eggshells. I always felt scared when I was in that house. I learned to become invisible in that house. Because I've always liked Star Wars, I thought I was becoming a Jedi Knight. Even then, God had blessed me with a resilient spirit. And I am grateful for that.

Because what was to follow in my life was going to be rough, sad, and painful, but it was for a purpose. I understand that today. I was about 10 or 11 when my dad kicked me out for slamming the metal screen door. I didn't know what to do, so I walked down the street to our neighborhood park. I just sat there on the bench. I started to cry, feeling scared and alone. At that moment, I hated God, myself, and everything. In my mind, I was just an unlovable, ugly kid with crooked teeth. But that was a lie because God doesn't make mistakes; He makes us all unique and to His liking, not ours. I wasn't born hating myself or having hate in my heart; that's something I learned from my parents. But God has taught me to love myself and love others. It's not always easy but I do my best. I strive for progress, not perfection.

Example: Oscar's "After version" for Chapter 1 of his story. These revisions allowed Oscar to quickly summarize his life growing up. He felt some of these teens would be able to relate to his situation. His chapter theme: God created you uniquely to His liking, and God doesn't make mistakes.

I grew up in a middle-class family; there were seven of us, and money was always tight. My dad was an abusive, angry alcoholic. He would beat me every chance he got and call me 'a worthless piece of crap' ever since I can remember. I honestly thought he hated me! When I was six years old, I started getting molested by a neighbor who happened to be my brother's best friend. I was scared to tell anybody, especially my parents, because I knew they would disown me.

I started to hate myself, wishing I'd been born to somebody else so that I could have parents that loved me. When my dad got angry, it would literally be a two- or three-day event. I would dread coming home because it would only be a matter of time before he would find a reason to get angry at me. I hated being at home because it felt like I was constantly walking on eggshells. Then the day came; I was about 11, and my dad kicked me out for slamming the metal screen door.

I didn't know what to do, so I walked down the street to our neighborhood park. I just sat there on the bench. I started to cry, feeling scared and alone. At that moment, I hated God, myself, and everything.

In my mind, I was just an unlovable, ugly kid with crooked teeth. But that was a lie because God doesn't make mistakes; He makes us all unique and to His liking, not ours. I wasn't born hating myself or having hate in my heart—that is something that I learned to do from my parents. But God has taught me to love myself and love others. It's not always easy, but I do my best. I strive for progress, not perfection.

Oscar has continued to refine his story and adjust it for different audiences and timeframes. You will do the same with your story. It will be much easier to adapt to different listeners and settings once you have put in the effort to create a manageable story.

There are a few additional things that can help you to release unnecessary details. For each chapter, start by asking yourself:

- What do I most want the listener to leave thinking about or focused on with this chapter?
- How do the details I plan to share support that?
- How do those detail(s) relate to God's influence on me and/or for them?

Considering these questions helps to keep you focused on what the listener will think about your story. This makes it easier for you to let go of things that don't support your points at this time or with these specific listeners.

One thing I often tell my clients is, *"Whatever does not add, dilutes."* Meaning that if a detail does not add to enhancing understanding or providing clarity, it could potentially dilute your message because your audience is distracted with a detail that is not relevant to the point you are making.

Another option to help you get the right amount of details for your listeners is to write what you think is pertinent to your story and share it with a Christian friend or mentor, asking them what was most helpful and interesting and what could be left out to help streamline your story. Let them know you are trying to shorten and focus your story and what your theme is. Keep an open mind to their feedback.

Create Connections That Build Momentum

To deliver a cohesive story, you want to consider how you will create connections that will build momentum for your listeners along the way. Two ways to do that are to be intentional with transitions and to use examples, analogies, and lessons learned.

Connect with Transitions

Transitions are the links you make between your chapters that give your story continuity. This is a way of making the connection for listeners between one chapter within your story and the next chapter. When transitions are missing between chapters, your story can feel choppy, confusing, or potentially aimless.

Some example transitions:

- Use a Question (often a rhetorical question is used).
  - "Are you wondering how this impacted my faith?"
  - "If you were in this situation, what would you be thinking?"
- Make a statement or use a statistic.
  - "Even then, God had blessed me with a resilient spirit. And I am grateful for that. Because what was to follow in my life was going to be rough, sad, and painful, but it was for a purpose—I understand that today."
  - "You can imagine we had another statistic working against us—2%—that's the statistic for getting pregnant at age 44."
- Link to your next point in the story.

- "Now that you understand... it would be good to know..."
- "The Lord gave me a new calling, helping me deal with a new life without my wife."

- Share a preview of what's coming next.
  - "Next, I will share what it's really like to be a gang leader."
  - "I can't talk about all 300 ministries, but I can highlight a few known to many of you. Let me showcase a few."
  - "I worked on a lot of different patterns that made me a tyrant, and I learned five valuable lessons that I want to share with you."

When you are mindful to make these connections for your listeners, it helps to keep them engaged because they can easily follow the story.

Keep Engagement As You Unfold Your Story

Keeping engagement while sharing your story can be achieved by tapping into many of the same ideas shared to open your story. When you share short stories, examples, or lessons learned along the way within your story, it gives you the ability to anchor your message, re-engage your listeners, or bring them into the next part of your story with purpose.

A few examples that were not shared in Chapter 8, *Openings that Engage*, are:

Lessons learned: Sometimes our stories involve lessons we learned, steps taken, or guidance from the Lord that can also be helpful for our listeners. Ciara and I both incorporated this idea into our testimonies that you read about in Chapter 5: *Outline Your Story*.

Example: When Ciara shared the five lessons she learned during her process out of rebellion, it was very helpful to her audience of teens and parents and gave them something tangible to leave thinking about.

Her five lessons:

1. Be vulnerable.
2. Take Responsibility
3. Know It's a Process
4. Accept Help
5. Family Love & Support Make a Difference

Example: In my testimony I share the five C's criteria that the Lord put on my heart for what to look for to meet a Godly man while dating. Many people have shared with me that hearing this list caused them to want to seek God's guidance for themselves.

1. Christian
2. Compatible
3. Communication
4. Commitment
5. Chemistry

Story: Sometimes referring to a third person's experience that is related to your story can provide an added perspective or encouragement for your listeners.

Example: Richard's story about his wife Libby's attitude during her cancer journey.

> Libby witnessed her life's journey and love for Jesus to everyone, especially those undergoing cancer treatments with her at the cancer centers.

They were amazed at her zest for life and love for the Lord. They were encouraged and gained hope after hearing everything she was doing while they were trying to cope. She lived her life to the fullest! She taught me to do the same.

Provide a New Perspective: When you can share a new perspective on something that is familiar to listeners, it can re-engage them along with providing an "Aha" moment.

Example: Chau gave her listeners at the industry conference a reason to pause and reflect on their own lives with this example and analogy.

> I learned that there's a significant difference between being driven and being ambitious. Being driven is to pursue and chase a result at all costs. It's analogous to a police officer chasing a criminal to get him off the streets to keep citizens safe. But in his pursuit, he doesn't notice the mom and son he ran over with his car, the grandmother he shot with his stray bullets, or the group of children who had to jump out of the way as he shot past them. He is focused on getting the criminal off the streets at all costs— good intentions, but with high costs and high casualties.

> Alternatively, being ambitious is to be clear about the desired end result while taking all costs into account. The short-, mid-, and long-term ripple effects on oneself and others. Take an honest look at yourself. Are you driven or ambitious?

I wonder if there is someone here who is waiting for the applause of the wrong person or the wrong people like I was five years ago? Some of us are doing things and living life to impress people who aren't even paying attention.

Sometimes, we get so addicted to the approval of others that we can't receive approval from God or ourselves. That was the woman I was five years ago.

You have just made it through the hardest part—the body of your story!

Because this is where we live our story daily, it can be the hardest to distill down to something manageable and easy for our listeners to take in. Yet, when you put these ideas into practice, you will find it getting easier and easier to share your story in a way that impacts your listeners' hearts and lives.

Now, it's time to invite them into God's bigger story.

Chapter 10

Invite Them Into God's Bigger Story

The closing is a special time to connect your message of hope to the opportunity for your listeners to connect with God at a deeper level or to receive the grace that He is extending to them through you. Your listeners want to know God is for them as well as for you. The closing is an opportunity to complete the story for both you and your listeners.

Up to this point you have provided your listeners an inspiring story of love, hope, and faith as you have personally experienced it. Now you have reached the point in your story where you can invite them into God's bigger story or take the next natural step.

As a way to determine what to include in your closing, ask yourself what you want to leave your listeners thinking about, challenged by, or invited into. When you take time to consider that and incorporate it into your closing, then your listeners will feel your story has ended with intention and purpose.

Your closing may include:

- Summarizing your story points
- Anchoring your main message
- Extending an invitation to take the next appropriate step based on your listener(s) and setting.

Your closing with an individual will likely be different than with a group. With an individual, it will largely depend on your relationship and how the conversation has gone thus far as to what is the next appropriate step to take with them.

Extending An Invitation to Know Jesus

If you feel led by the Holy Spirit to invite your listener into a relationship with Jesus, and they want to accept that invitation, you can lead them in a simple prayer such as this:

> "Lord Jesus, thank You for showing me how much I need You. Thank You for dying on the cross for me. Please forgive all my failures and the sins of my past. Make me clean and help me start fresh with You. I now receive You into my life as my Lord and Savior. Help me to love and serve You with all my heart. Amen."

The Pocket Testament League provided this example of a prayer for salvation. They also give these three simple steps for accepting Christ that you can share with them:

1. Admit you are a sinner and turn away from sin (John 8:11, NIV).

2. Believe (have faith) that when Jesus died on the cross, He took the punishment for all your sin, and He rose to life again to conquer death (John 1:29, NIV).

3. Receive (ask) Jesus Christ as your Lord and Savior. *To all who received Him, to those who believed in His name, He gave the right to become children of God* (John 1:12, NIV).

The Pocket Testament League is an international ministry currently providing resources in over 100 countries. Their mission is to mobilize and equip Christians to read, carry, and share the word of God. They can provide several free resources that give you other approaches and language for this conversation, along with learning more about the Bible and being a follower of Christ. This information can be found on their website: www.ptl.org.

Only God Can Convict the Heart

As much as we desire to bring our friends into relationship with Christ, Paul reminds us that we cannot convict the heart—only God can.

> *"As the Lord assigned the task. I planted the seed, Apollos watered it, but God made it grow"* (1 Corinthians 3:5–6, NIV).

As Bob Shank shares in The Master's Program, "Most Christians feel like they are incapable of harvest (evangelism), so they never fully engage the process of cultivation, planting, weeding, and watering."

In reflecting on this, I realized I had not been fully engaging in opportunities to share my story because I thought I had to do it all. I have since learned that God wants and needs the full body of Christ to help the lost become His.

We are called to share our experience of Christ, the change He has made in our lives, and be willing to be used by God to open hearts and minds to a relationship with Him through our story. He assures us that the Holy Spirit is at work, even if we don't see that in the moment.

Examples of Closings

How you ultimately choose to complete your story is similar to how you open your story—it will depend on your personal style, your listeners, and the setting. It will also depend on how you feel the Holy Spirit has been guiding you to close your story. When you seek His guidance both in advance as part of preparing your close and in the moment when sharing your story, He will show you what is best for your listeners.

I think it is worth restating that when we are willing to prepare our story in advance, it frees us up in the moment to hear the Holy Spirit's guidance for the natural next steps to take with our listeners.

Let's come back to Laura and Oscar to look at a couple of examples of closings.

Example: Laura's closing section of her five-minute testimony:

> For 21 years, I have been living as a beloved daughter of God. I am forgiven. I am secure. Life hurts me sometimes. Memories hurt me sometimes. But I am not alone. I am His. And I am at rest. I am fully known and fully loved. I am grateful.
>
> Sin carries us away from God. But I want to tell you that the One who created you wants you back. He is calling you. He is holding out full forgiveness and new life as His. Only turn in His direction, and He will run to you, like the father of the prodigal son. Turn to Him. Accept the gift of forgiveness He is holding out for you. It is only a prayer away.

Laura's closing focused on what God wants for her listeners personally and that it is only one prayer away for them to receive it.

Example: Oscar's closing:

> Never think that you're alone—you are some-body and have God, and even though we might not know each other, I'm rooting for you, too. Today, I have a purpose: to bring the message of hope and God's love to anybody who will listen.
>
> I'm not saying that life will be a fairytale because it won't. As you know, life can some-times be hard and beat you to the point of giving up. But don't do it! Don't give up on your dreams! I hope you shoot for the highest star because even if you miss, you'll hit the star just below it, which is still pretty amazing. If you fall ten times, get up eleven times. We are all good at something. Figuring it out is your job. I had to walk through fire to find my joy and purpose in life.
>
> Let me share one last significant number with you: 43:11. That is the Bible Scripture Isaiah 43:11, the verse God used to open my eyes to His saving grace and the verse that inspired me to want to help you. That is why I created the Firewalkers Ministry—to give you options and to help you find your purpose and joy.
>
> Here is what you can start with. Join me next Tuesday after school as we launch our Firewalkers success program. We'll help you find what you are good at.

> I have seen God's hand on my life, and even though I felt the heat of the flames, it was God's grace that refused to let me burn up. I have to remind myself that no matter how hard times get, it's only temporary, but God's love and grace are eternal. Thank you for your time, I appreciate it.

Oscar anchored his message with one last significant number, Isaiah 43:11, and then invited these students to take a small step to attend a meeting after school where they could learn more. This was the appropriate next step based on his audience and setting.

Expect Multiple Drafts as You Hone Your Story

We live in a "one draft" world, or at least it feels that way! Somewhere along the way, our culture decided that good things could or should be achieved the first time—that there is an unspoken rule that we are not good enough if it takes several tries to get to a good testimony story. That is rarely the case.

If you feel anxious about needing to take several tries at establishing your outline and organizing your testimony details, know that you are not alone. That's part of the natural process of getting to a story that suits your style and honors God.

Often, it is the journey to getting there that God had in mind all along, drawing you closer to Him as you reflect on all that He has done in your life.

It's important to realize that it may take several drafts to get your story to a place that feels comfortable for you to share it with confidence and flexibility. Continue to pray and seek the Holy Spirit's guidance. Also, know that your story will develop and change as you share it. That's a good thing!

Closing Thoughts on Organizing Your Story

In the journey of sharing our faith, organization is not meant to be a constraint. It's the gateway to connection. By mapping your spiritual journey, outlining your story, and structuring the details, you are creating a path for your audience to follow, making sure they gain the most out of your story while enhancing your connection with them.

So, embrace structure and see it as a key to unlocking the transformational potential of your story. Remember, structure helps to keep things moving in a way that allows the relationship to remain the focal point. Keep this perspective as you read the next chapter, where you'll learn how to personalize your story for your listeners.

PART 4

Value Your Audience

Chapter 11

Personalize Your Story for Your Audience

Susan invited me to lunch. She was excited to share her involvement with a college-focused Christian Ministry and all the things they are doing at the local campuses to make Jesus known. Her enthusiasm was refreshing, and I was interested to learn more.

About 20 minutes into our time together, I started to feel disengaged. Susan knew we had a daughter who would soon be going off to college, so I was surprised that she hadn't asked about or referenced our daughter's college situation yet.

Susan was unaware that she was missing an opportunity to engage with me at a level that would turn this into a relational conversation, not just an informational one. Susan's intent was coming from a good place. She just didn't realize the value of bringing her listener into her story.

We can all relate to a one-sided conversation like this. Whether it happens with an individual or in a group setting, a one-sided conversation cannot fully engage our hearts and minds in the way a two-way conversation does.

We want our listeners to feel seen and valued when we share our stories. We want them to feel that our story has implications for them. It's the reason we are sharing it.

Within this principle of *Value Your Audience*, we'll explore going beyond considering who will be listening to your story to how to personalize your story in a way that creates connections with your listeners as you unfold your story.

Finding the Sweet Spot for Your Listeners

To maximize the impact of sharing your faith story, it is important to realize there are three stories involved when you share your story or messages as a Christian.

> *Your Story*: The unique life story you have lived. This includes the relationship you have with Jesus and the role He has played in your faith journey.
>
> *God's Story*: We desire to make God known. He is the hero of our story. When we share the good news of the gospel and how He is working in and through our lives, we are helping to make Jesus known and relevant to our listeners.
>
> *Audience's Story*: When you personalize your story for your listeners, the story becomes relevant to them, enhancing engagement, connections, and your relationship with them.

When you are intentional about integrating all three of these stories as part of the telling of your story, this is called the "Sweet Spot." When you are mindful of integrating these three, it creates an added level of engagement for your listeners.

Within this chapter, we'll look at four audience engagement tools—simple ways to build stronger connections with your listeners so that you can authentically connect with and include them as you unfold your story, finding the Sweet Spot for them.

The Power of Personalization: Making Your Story Relevant to Others

In my experience, the most forgotten story is the audience's story. Speakers tend to speak *at* their audience versus *with* their audience. This is not ideal for relationship building! At times, speakers may not even acknowledge their listeners as they share their story. This can lead to a disengaged audience.

You don't want that. After all, the reason you are sharing your story is to benefit them—to encourage and inspire them to greater hope and faith and to know Jesus.

What does it do for you as a listener when you feel valued?

For most people, it opens their hearts and minds to the person speaking and what is being said. The story takes on relevance and connects them personally to the speaker and message.

An effective communicator will always personalize their story to the purpose, needs, and language of their audience. Begin by asking yourself a few questions about your listeners so that you can further personalize the story with them in mind:

- What is their point of reference with faith/religion?
- What is important to them right now?
- What are they concerned about?
- What do they expect or need at this time?
- If speaking to a group, what brought them together? Is there a purpose for you to share your story with them at this time?

- Given the above, what do they need to know or not know?

I suggest you also return to your relationship prayer journal. As you sought God's guidance for your story, did He show you anything about your listeners and their needs that you can now consider incorporating into your interaction with them?

Reflecting on these questions and God's guidance from your prayer journal will help you gain a better understanding of your audience's mindset and begin to consider how to personalize your story with them in mind.

Before I introduce you to the four engagement tools, let's look at how Jesus modeled this for us.

How Jesus Engaged His Listeners

We can learn from Jesus on how to engage our listeners, as seen through the story of the woman at the well. As you read the following passages from John 4:4–26 (NIV), consider how He interacted with her.

The story begins with Jesus needing to go through Samaria. As He does, He becomes tired and sits down by a well. We'll pick up the story there.

> "When the Samaritan woman came to draw water, Jesus said to her, '*Will you give Me a drink?*'
>
> The Samaritan woman said to Him, '*You are a Jew and I am a Samaritan woman. How can You ask me for a drink?*'
>
> Jesus answered her, '*If you knew the gift of God and Who it is that asks you for a drink, you*

would have asked Him and He would have given you living water.'

'*Sir,*' the woman said, '*You have nothing to draw with and the well is deep. Where can You get this living water? Are You greater than our father Jacob, who gave us this well and drank from it himself, as did also his sons and his flocks and herds?*'

Jesus answered, '*Everyone who drinks this water will be thirsty again, but whoever drinks the water I give him will never thirst. Indeed, the water I give him will become in him a spring of water welling up to eternal life.*'

The woman said to him, '*Sir, give me this water so that I won't get thirsty and have to keep coming here to draw water.*'

He told her, '*Go, call your husband and come back.*'

'*I have no husband,*' she replied.

Jesus said to her, '*You are right when you say you have no husband. The fact is, you have had five husbands, and the man you now have is not your husband. What you have just said is quite true.*'

'*Sir,*' the woman said, '*I can see that You are a prophet. Our fathers worshiped on this mountain, but you Jews proclaim that the place where we must worship is in Jerusalem.*'

Jesus declared, '*Believe Me, woman, a time is coming when you will worship the Father neither on this mountain nor in Jerusalem. You Samaritans worship what you do not know; we worship what we do know, for salvation is from the Jews. Yet a time is coming and has come when the true worshippers will worship the Father in spirit and truth, for they are the kind of worshippers the Father seeks. God is Spirit, and His worshippers must worship in spirit and in truth.*'

The woman said, '*I know that Messiah (called Christ) is coming. When He comes, He will explain everything to us.*'

Then Jesus declared, '*I who speaks to you am He.*'

Then the disciples returned…

Then, leaving her water jar, the woman went back to town and said to the people, *'Could this be the Christ?'* They came out of the town and made their way toward him."

What Jesus Modeled for Us

In this interaction, we see Jesus talk to her with an attitude of love, without condemnation. He goes on to interact with her in a way that engages her personally.

1. He talks to her with respect and **asks her a question:**

"Will you give me a drink?" (Simple, yet acknowledges *He sees her.*)

Jesus talks to her about how to achieve eternal life. He offers hope and not condemnation.

2. He shares the gospel message with her in an **inclusive** way:

"*Everyone* who drinks this water will be thirsty again, but *whoever* drinks the water I give him will never thirst. Indeed, the water I give him will become in him a spring of water welling up to eternal life."

This gives her a vision of a future that includes and impacts her.

3. He **references her specific situation:**

"Go, call your husband and come back."

"I have no husband."

"You are right when you say you have no husband. The fact is, you have five husbands."

He knows this and yet is unfazed by her sin. Instead, He acknowledges her situation.

4. She becomes a witness, saying, "Could this be the Christ?" **She invites** the village people to come meet Jesus. As a result, they went to see Him.

Jesus valued her, interacted with her, loved her, and offered her a way to eternal life. This conversation established a relationship that had an eternal impact and demonstrated that she was valued.

Four Audience Engagement Tools

We desire to include our listeners in a meaningful way. Yet, we may not always be sure of how to do that. The insights gained from how Jesus engaged the woman at the well can also be modeled in our own stories.

Jesus starts with an attitude of love and encourages us to do the same. When your starting place is from an authentic, caring heart for your audience, it creates connections that you can build on when interacting with them.

These four simple ways of engaging your listeners are intended to provide you with some ideas that you can use to help connect your story in a meaningful way with your listeners.

1. Ask Questions

Asking questions leads to getting to know your listeners better and helps you to personalize your story with their responses in mind. Questions engage the mind and draw upon their own past experiences or ask them to consider something. Even when the question is rhetorical, it gets the listeners thinking about their responses.

- If you were in that situation, what would you be thinking?
- Have you ever thought about…?
- How many of us are doing, saying, and engaging in things because it looks good?
- Do you ever feel that way?
- What's been your experience with religion?
- How do you think God is wanting to lead you through this?

When asking questions, you want to be sure to pause after you have asked them. If the question is rhetorical, give them a few seconds to absorb the question and form a response in their minds. If you want an actual response to the question, maintain eye contact and wait a few seconds so that they can decide the answer and then offer it up to you. You may need to repeat the question to let them know you would like a response.

2. Use Inclusive Language

Inclusive language is a way to speak *with* your audience rather than *at* your audience. It says to your listeners, "This is also about you." It's another opportunity to acknowledge their experiences as part of a group, community, or cause and bring them into the conversation.

- As parents, most of us can relate to…
- As Christians, we desire to…
- If you have ever lost someone, you may agree…
- If you have ever been on a college campus, you may have seen…
- Like you, I am a Barnabas member because…
- Is there someone here waiting for the applause of the wrong person, the wrong people, like I was five years ago?
- Every one of us is called to be heroic for God's Kingdom…

3. Reference Them and/or Their Situation

We all like to be acknowledged, and the more specifically that is done, the more drawn in we become to listen as audience members.

- When you went to (college, Europe, etc.), what was your experience?
- Given you just went through (challenge or trial), what are your concerns?

- Knowing you (this group), I have observed…
- This congregation has demonstrated its commitment to…
- Last week, you mentioned…

In Matthew 5, within the Sermon on the Mount, Jesus intentionally began many of His points by putting His audience into the situation by starting with "You or Anyone."

- *You* are the salt of the earth…
- *You* are the light of the world...
- *You* have heard it said long ago…
- *Anyone* who says to his brother…

4. Invite Them to Take a Next Step

As the Holy Spirit guides you, consider if there is a natural question, approach, or next step to invite them into.

- I invite you to join us for a campus prayer walk.
- Would you like to know more about…
- A small step could be…
- Would you like to know Jesus personally?

As you learned, at the heart of every story lies the power to connect, inspire, and transform our listeners' hearts and minds when we value them and invite them into God's bigger story. Your story can be a vehicle to facilitate that happening when you are intentional about finding the "Sweet Spot" and incorporating the audience's story within your story.

Use the four engagement tools as modeled by Jesus to help you create or enhance your connection with your listeners as you unfold your story.

You've got this! Now, it's time to prepare to deliver your story with confidence.

Example: Erin Weidemann's Story: Inspiring a movement using the four engagement tools.

Context: Erin is on a mission to inspire a movement! She wants to engage people in joining efforts to share stories about women of the Bible as role models for young girls. She and her husband, Brent, founded a company called Bible Belles. They produce books and resources focused on introducing young girls to these female heroes of the Bible.

They reached a point in the ministry where they desired to amplify their message to a broader audience. Erin was asked to deliver a keynote speech to a professional Christian organization called The Barnabas Group. There were 400+ people in attendance, primarily businessmen and women.

Her keynote speech focused on three key outcomes embodied in the "Value Your Audience" guiding principles:

- Connect the Bible Belles ministry story to the audience's personal and organizational mission.
- Emphasize and demonstrate the audience's ability to make a difference.
- Organize the content so that key messages stand out and inspire the audience.

Below, I provide the full script (versus an outline) so that you can read how Erin used the four engagement tools to include her audience and invite them into God's bigger story—one that has eternal impact.

Heroes for the Kingdom

Opening

A special thank you to Jim West and the leadership team at The Barnabas Group for inviting me to be with you.

Before becoming the co-founder and creator of Bible Belles, a full-time writer and speaker, I spent almost ten years as an educator—both in public and private schools with kids of various backgrounds, abilities, and experiences, mostly English. And because I taught language and writing classes, I have spent countless hours poring over stories—short stories and other literary works, epic poetry, libraries of novels, narrative fiction, and the real-life accounts of people and their adventures.

Since God breathed His story and its characters into existence, we have been drawn to the stories of heroes—like firefighters who run into buildings when everyone else is running out; we are captivated and inspired by brave souls who stand up for justice, warriors who fight for causes worth fighting for—because heroes do not do what they do for recognition, credit, or fame. They do it because, on a small, medium, or large scale, they can take something wrong and set it right.

Isn't it interesting that when we read the stories of heroes, sometimes we don't consider ourselves in the same category? We are just doing life, and maybe we've started to ask some of the right questions:

Inclusive Language

Use of Questions

- *Why am I here?*
- *What is the unique value you called me to provide this world?*
- *What are my gifts, and who are they for?*
- *How can I shine the light of Jesus into a dark and broken world?*
- *God, how do you want to use me?*
- *What work do you have for me that will reveal more of You to the world?*

And then God presents an opportunity that leads us to take the answers to those important questions and put them into action. He's already created these moments and seasons of life for us to inhabit. Because the truth is that…

Inclusive Language

Every one of us is called to be heroic for God's Kingdom.

I'd like to spend our time this evening sharing with you a little bit more about the journey God has taken us on and invite you to search your heart for the ways God is calling you to be a hero in His story."

Invitation

Chapter 1: Girls Need Real Heroes

I was first diagnosed with cancer when I was 26. I had walked a painful path as a young girl, struggling with what I later realized is a universal struggle that all girls face—insecurity, comparison, and trying to measure up to the world's standard of beauty.

I grew up in your typical 'check the box' church experience and never really understood what it meant to have a relationship with Jesus. I stopped walking with the Lord when I was 16, and it was ten years later—26 years old, diagnosed with an aggressive form of cancer in my neck, head, and chest—when I found myself on the floor of my parent's bathroom during a 72-hour quarantine for radiation treatment, sobbing, asking Jesus that if He was real, could He come and help me? Before that moment, I had never (and I mean never) prayed and really believed that there was a God who existed and who was listening.

I eventually got out of that room and thought, *Well, I'm going to die.* And for the very first time in my life, I asked the right questions—"God, what was I created to do? How do You want me to spend the time I have left?" I felt a stirring in my soul for kids, so I went back to school, got my credentials, and began my career.

The more time I spent with kids in and out of the classroom and on the athletic field, the more my heart began to break for the next generation of girls. Watching them completely misunderstand who they were created to be, caring more about how they look than how they love. It was then that I began to realize God wanted something done about it.

We first had the idea for Bible Belles on the way home from church. Brent and I were debating/arguing about what to get our niece, Hannah, for her birthday. She was five at the time. We wanted our gift to mean something, not be just another toy. So we thought, there is a great story about Hannah in the Bible. Why don't *we* make her a storybook so she can know she shares her name with this great, godly woman, and it's got this awesome lesson about prayer and trusting God's plan? We thought, *Okay, let's do it!*

So I write the story, Brent illustrates the cover. We have it bound at Kinko's, wrap it up, and give it to her—and she's confused. 'Auntie Erin, I didn't know a Hannah was in the Bible.' That sweet little girl couldn't name *any* women of the Bible—but she could tell the name and details of every Disney princess.

We had our *aha* moment—what if there was a way we could connect girls to *real heroes*—the women in Scripture, women whose inner beauty God used in powerful ways, women whose stories can repair a girl's broken way of thinking about herself and her place in the world.

And what if we could do it in a way that competes with all of the high-quality brands like Disney and Pixar? If we're truly competing for our kids, we have to compete on the same level as the rest of the world.

To change culture, content creation must shift so that the end goal isn't mindless entertainment: it's an eternity mindset.

Use of Questions →

So we got going. We didn't know where to start, and it didn't exactly feel heroic—but God doesn't need our expertise, does He? He simply needs our obedience.

Chapter 2: The Sound of the Belles Will Be H.E.A.R.D.

When we first started out, we did it because the world has a lot to tell girls about beauty. They are hit on all sides by this constant barrage of messaging. This noise tells them, 'Here's what you have to be to be beautiful. Here's what you must do, say, and change about yourself to gain love and acceptance. You should care more about how you look than how you love people. Don't seek God's appointments. Seek the approval of others.' And the world is wrong, but it is *loud*!

I started researching the women of the Bible and prayed *hard* for which women to include. As a teacher, it made sense to take girls on a journey, a progression that would start with absolutely no relationship with the Lord and develop five specific character traits to prepare them to step boldly into His plan and their purpose.

That would start with prayer. The first step in a real relationship with God is to pray. To open your life to Him takes open and honest communication. That's why Hannah is the *belle of prayer.*

Next is patience—because once you're talking to the Lord, the next step is to learn to sit, be still, and wait patiently to discern His voice and act according to His timing. That's why Esther is the *belle of patience.*

Abigail is the *belle of bravery*—because once your relationship is established, it's sure to be tested. Our kids need to know that they can call upon the courage of God to make the right choices because He is always with them.

And that's right where the story takes a turn, away from self and toward others. Because we are called to love God and love others faithfully, to put God's will and the needs of others ahead of our own desires. That's why Ruth is the *belle of loyalty.*

Prayer. Patience. Bravery. Loyalty. Once a little girl realizes she can aim for and possess these four pillars of character, she will be ready to step into her unique leadership role in God's kingdom. She will learn that being a leader is more than having the wisdom to know what needs to be done. A true leader can stir action in herself and others. That's why Deborah, the fifth and final belle in the series, is the *belle of leadership.*

It wasn't until I put them in that order that I realized their initials—Hannah, Esther, Abigail, Ruth, and Deborah. Their initials spell the word HEARD. In a world where millions of little girls are told they need to be beautiful and that they need to earn their worth, what an incredible opportunity we have to show them that their voices matter. The Lord is calling them to go out into the world and be heard—to use their voices for God and for good.

Chapter 3: Raising Kingdom Heroes Will Take A Village

In the time we went from ideation to creation, Brent and I became parents to a sweet girl, but you don't have to be parents to care deeply about the next generation.

I'm a five-time cancer survivor, and with my medical history, I never expected to become a mother.

Reference Audience →

And I'm learning that what people say is true—it takes a village to raise a child. And it's going to take a village of Kingdom builders—like the men and women in this room today...

Who will activate their gifts to create this culture shift to enable God's message about how He feels about girls and boys to the far corners of the world and

Invitation

prepare them to carry that message into the future—to be the voices of the future?

I'd like to invite you tonight to come alongside and help us to amplify the message—to help us create partnerships that get these resources into the hands of children all over the world. We have plans to be a major player in content creation, delivery, and distribution so that we can compete with the big players out there.

Invitation

Specific asks we have are for people to come alongside to help us compete on a global level with this message: for little girls to grow up and become a powerful source for His Kingdom, and not just for girls in the United States who have parents and resources to give these girls.

This is a global message that needs to reach every single girl who has ears to hear it!

Our big dreams include multi-language translation, global distribution of curriculum, animation, and other media content that can be used in a powerful way.

If this sounds intriguing to you, our sign-in sheet is on page 41. There are specific ways to get involved.

Closing

In closing… heroes do not do what they do for recognition, credit, or fame. They do it because they can take something wrong and set it right again. And that's my challenge to you this evening.

Invitation

That's what I'd like to invite you to this evening. To share in the opportunity, we have to give every girl what she needs—real heroes so she can discover the hero inside herself.

To take a little wrong that exists out in the world and set it right. To join in what the Lord is doing to build His Kingdom here on earth and to proclaim the ultimate hero of God's story—His son, Jesus Christ.

Thank you so much, and I can't wait to connect with some of you later this evening."

Outcome:

Erin's use of questions, inclusive language, and her invitation to participate personalized this keynote in a way that resonated with her audience. The audience was inspired and engaged and, as a result, many key introductions were made. People were inspired to help share their message and buy the books for the girls in their lives.

Erin has gone on to do more speaking engagements, including being featured on CBS, CNN, NBC, and World Vision. She and Brent have expanded the business to include podcasts, videos, stories for boys, and other related resources. They can be found at www.truthbecomesher.com.

You don't need to deliver a keynote speech to model the use of these four engagement tools for Valuing Your Audience— any of them can help you to authentically connect with your listeners, whether in a one-to-one or group setting.

PART 5

Enjoy Sharing Confidently

Chapter 12
The Five P's that Lead to Confidence

Can you remember a time when someone's story truly inspired you? When it caused you to think differently about your own life, or take a step of faith, or change a course of action?

That was the Holy Spirit in action! God worked through that person who was willing to share their story with you. Look at what a difference that made for you! God wants you to be able to do that for your circle of influence—to expect and embrace opportunities where you can have that kind of impact.

But what stands in the way of sharing your story at that moment?

What often stands in our way is nervousness. We all experience nervousness when preparing to share an important message or testimony. It's one way to realize we cannot make an impact without God's help.

The good news is that God has provided tools for overcoming our nervousness. We would be remiss not to tap into them in our efforts to glorify Him.

God Chooses the Ordinary to Do the Extraordinary

You may doubt your ability to share your story effectively, fearing rejection or inadequacy, or feeling unqualified or unprepared for what God has called you to do. Rest assured, this is a natural feeling, and God has shown us throughout the Bible that He uses ordinary people to do extraordinary things for His Kingdom purposes.

In the Bible, we learn about people who, like you and me, may have felt unqualified or unprepared for God's call. People who, despite their weaknesses, fear of speaking, or imperfections, were able to make a Kingdom difference. God could provide what they needed when they needed it to accomplish His purposes.

They were willing to take steps of faith, even if afraid, and we can learn from these extraordinary examples. Several of these brave people are found in Hebrews 11, also known as the *Hall of Faith.*

Here are a few of these heroes of the faith, along with how they may have felt unqualified or unprepared:

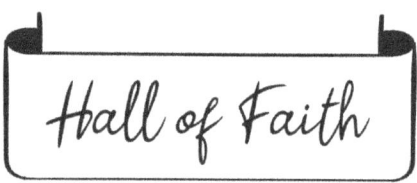

- Moses had a temper and stuttered.
- Gideon had low self-esteem.
- Abraham was fearful and old.
- David was an adulterer with family issues.
- Rahab experienced the shame of prostitution.

It is inspiring to see that extraordinary things happen when God chooses to move through ordinary people. In his best-selling book, *The Purpose Driven Life,* Pastor Rick Warren observes that God chooses to use human weakness to show His power.

Flawed and ordinary people like Moses, David, and Gideon were chosen and empowered by God to accomplish His magnificent purposes. Warren shares:

> This is why God wants to use your weaknesses, not just your strengths. If all people see are your strengths, they get discouraged and think, "Well, good for them, but I'll never be able to do that." But when they see God using you in spite of your weaknesses, it encourages them to think, "Maybe God can use me!"[13]

God Wants to Shift Our Attention from Our Messiness to His Message and Purposes

When we are afraid to communicate our story, then our own discomfort becomes the focus. When we concentrate on what God wants us to share with our listeners, they become the focal point. Warren concludes:

> Our strengths create competition, but our weaknesses create community. At some point in your life, you must decide whether you want to impress people or influence people.

One of the greatest traits of an influencer is vulnerability. Rick Warren speaks to a level of vulnerability that can connect your listener to your story in a way that facilitates the Holy Spirit to touch their hearts.

Remember that the impact or outcomes of sharing our story is not in our hands; it is the work of the Holy Spirit. Our part is to be vulnerable (not seen as perfect) and to step past our

---

[13] Rick Warren. *The Purpose Driven Life*: Zondervan 2002, page 277.

fears and nervousness so that God can use our story for His purposes.

God has provided tools to help us harness our nervousness in our efforts to glorify Him. We can gain confidence by applying them to deliver our stories.

Getting Past My Own Nervousness

When I was asked to share my testimony at the Christian women's event, I felt an extra surge of nervousness with this specific group. I felt God was asking me to share my sin story with them, and I had only done that publicly one other time at my church.

Here's the thing: when it's *your* sin story, it often carries an extra weight of nerves and the feelings of potential judgment and shame that come from it, even when we know Jesus has already forgiven and redeemed us. That bold step into vulnerability can often be the hardest to take.

I needed to harness my negative self-talk and get deliberate about praying for God's peace, knowing He had guided me to share this part of my story with this audience. I re-read my relationship prayer journal for this event, which helped me calm my nerves and trust that the Holy Spirit was guiding my efforts.

I organized and prepared what I wanted to say; now, it was time to practice saying it. I invited my sister over to listen to me share it. I know the power of out-loud practice and its ability to help free us up to be ourselves.

It initially felt clunky but after sharing it multiple times, I was at a place to confidently share in the larger group setting. I was humbled and reminded that we all need to lean on God and use the tools He has provided to bring Him glory with our story.

God was faithful that day to show me the fruit of my investment in preparation and practicing. The group responded positively to my story. Many women came up to share how my story personally affected them.

One such person was a co-worker. I was initially apprehensive about inviting her to the event. But afterward, she shared with tears in her eyes that this was God's perfect timing for her to hear my story. Hearing how Jesus meets us in our struggles and loves us unconditionally gave her renewed hope and inspired her to reevaluate her faith. God's presence was felt, and I was grateful He allowed me to be a part of His movement with this group of women.

In the process of getting past my own nervousness, I tapped into what I call the Five P's that lead to confidence.

The Five P's that Lead to Confidence

1. Prayer: His Strength, His Love, His Outcomes

Just as you prayed for guidance before mapping and outlining your faith story, prayer is an essential step in preparing to deliver that story. As communicators of God's story, we want to continue acknowledging our dependence on Him, seeking His guidance, and aligning ourselves with His purposes as we prepare to share our story.

Seeking God's guidance throughout the process of preparing, practicing, and delivering your story will not only help you to personalize your story for your listeners, but it will also give you the confidence that you are delivering a message that will make a difference for them.

- Ask God to purify and prepare your heart so you can share your story from an attitude of love, grace, respect, and kindness.

- Ask God to prepare the hearts of your listeners. May they be attentive to the message and follow His Holy Spirit leading in response to your story.

- Ask the Holy Spirit, who is already at work within us, to empower you to do the good work He has for you.

- Pray for opportunities to share your story and for God to place divine appointments into your life.

As part of your prayers, consider selecting a few Scriptures to help you focus as you seek God's guidance. Below are a few Scriptures that I have found helpful to reference during my prayer time.

> *"May the words of my mouth and the*
> *meditation of my heart be pleasing to you,*
> *O LORD, my rock, and my redeemer"*
> (Psalm 19:14, NLT).

> *"Now to Him who is able to do immeasurably*
> *more than all we ask or imagine, according*
> *to His power that is at work within us, to Him*
> *be glory in the church and in Christ Jesus*
> *throughout all generations, forever and ever"*
> (Ephesians 3:20–21, NIV)!

2. Preparation: It's a Process. Plan on Revisions.

As much as we wish it wasn't true, preparation is a process, not an event. Preparation gives you the best opportunity to share a compelling story focused on your audience and frees you up to be guided by the Holy Spirit as you deliver your story.

It's helpful to remember that it may take several revisions to produce your story to suit your personal style, audience, and setting. It is normal to have several, if not many, versions of your outline, and ultimately your story, by the time you feel fully confident to share it in various settings.

This is your personal story; anticipate that it will change and evolve. This means you may not say it the same way each time you share it, nor should you. If your audience is changing, and the Holy Spirit is guiding you, then it is natural that you will adjust it in the moment.

As we work through the preparation process, it is also another way for us to relate to God and deepen our understanding of what He has done in and through us with our faith journey. God is often more concerned with taking us through the process with Him than getting to the end result.

3. Practice Enhances Confidence and Credibility.

Once you have prayed and prepared, it's time to practice, practice, practice. Practice not only enhances your confidence but also your relationship and credibility with your listeners. Your goal is not to come across as over-rehearsed but to deliver a clear story that listeners understand, leading to greater connection and credibility.

Setting aside time to practice your story will also free you to be yourself. When you are comfortable with what you want to say, it allows you to focus on your listeners and enables your personality to shine through.

Bottom line: perfection is not required. The combination of passion, organization, and an audience focus enhances your connection and credibility far more than the "perfect" move, gesture, words, or attire.

Remember, you are telling a very personal and important story. This matters! Please don't leave it up to chance.

Practicing out loud is best.

I recommend practicing out loud a minimum of three times. When you practice in your mind while reading your notes, your mind will tend to fill in the gaps where content may not naturally flow well. Practicing out loud allows you to work the kinks out and begin to really own your story.

I like to say, "Mary Ann does not show up until the third time out loud." What I mean by that is my personality doesn't shine through until I have practiced my story or message three times out loud.

- The first time, I determine if I like what I'm going to say. Are my points clear? Do my word choices work well? And so on.

- The second time, I determine if I am pausing for effect in the right places, whether the story flows well overall, etc. This also helps you work through tricky words and phrases, identify filler words, and determine if a transition is needed at certain points.

- The third time: I begin to feel like I own it and can bring more of my style into play—smile, embed remarks, and ask questions that add to the vividness of my story.

Practice frees you up to be you.

Once I have three practices under my belt, I will continue to practice as time permits. Continuing to practice builds my confidence and ultimately frees me up to be present for my listeners. Here are a few more ideas for practicing:

- Practice with people you know and are comfortable around: your friends, your spouse, or your church small group. This helps you to be conversational.

- Time yourself as you practice: this enables you to know how much time it takes to share your story. Most testimony stories are about three to five minutes long.

- Use notes as you build confidence. Bullet points versus paragraphs are most helpful if you choose to use notes. The outline template is a nice option to use as notes.

- Practice your opening: We are most nervous during our story's first one to two minutes, yet this is the least practiced part of any delivery. If time is limited, practicing just your opening several times can help you feel confident as you enter your story.

4. Proactive: Be Proactive with Managing Nervous Symptoms.

Most nervous symptoms we encounter can actually be managed if we are proactive. When you can proactively manage physical symptoms, it helps you feel more comfortable and confident to share your story. The goal here is to operate within your style. There is no perfect delivery to aspire to, only to avoid distracting behaviors and become comfortable delivering your story. That is what allows your passion and personality to shine through. The following can help you to be proactive with nervous symptoms.

Nervous Tension

- Breathe: Taking deep breaths allows your body to relax and your mind to engage.

- Self-talk: Become aware of what you are telling yourself as nerves increase. Try shifting your inner dialog to a positive statement like, "Jesus has given me a unique story to share," versus "My story isn't very interesting."

- Memorize Scripture: repeating the Word of God can quickly decrease your nervous tension and give you the confidence to share your story. When we internalize God's Word, we are putting to work the armor of God. Memorizing Scripture makes it easier to come to mind when needed. Having a few "go-to" Scriptures makes this easier.

> *"It is God who arms me with strength and makes my way perfect"* (Psalm 18:32, NLT).

> *"I can do all things through Christ who gives me strength"* (Philippians 4:13, NIV).

> *"For God did not give us a spirit of timidity, but a spirit of power, of love and self-discipline"* (2 Timothy 1:7, NLT).

Eye Contact

- Maintaining eye contact with your listener(s) builds rapport and makes it feel more conversational. If you are in a group setting, a best practice is to look at different individuals, holding your contact for three seconds to create a connection with them. In a smaller group you'll want to eventually look at everyone.

- When you have asked your listener(s) a question, maintain eye contact and pause to demonstrate you want to hear their response.

Voice Pace, Projection and Filler Words

- Pace: When you speak too fast, it causes your listeners to have to work to take in your story. Try to maintain a conversational pace. Think conversational versus formal, as this facilitates helping you show up with your natural pace and style.

- When speaking to a group, slowing your pace down by 30% can also help them receive your information better, especially with multi-language or older audiences.

- Consider the power of the pause to help you slow down with purpose. A purposeful pause is also a good way to emphasize a point you want to stand out.

- Speaking too slowly can also be a distraction. It can seem like you're searching for your words or need more preparation. Searching for words on occasion is fine. If you are uncertain how your pace impacts your delivery and engagement, ask a friend to give you feedback.

- Voice projection and volume usually come into play if you are speaking in a larger group setting or on a stage. Request the use of a microphone if you have been asked to share your story in a large group setting. Most venues that host groups can make that available.

- Filler words—such as "um," "you know," "aha," "basically," "like," and "actually"—can be a distraction or even change the meaning of your message. To greatly reduce filler words and awkward pauses, consider whether you can use an intentional transition instead.

- Transitions are what you say to bridge one idea to another. You'll want to determine and practice transitions because filler words are the brain's natural mechanism for "filling in the gap." The unintended consequence of not thinking through and creating transitions will be the overuse of filler words, awkward pauses, or random comments.

- Limit use of Jargon: As Christians, we have our own language, or "Christianese" as some call it, that we use without thinking about it. In our community, this works well when communicating with each other. If we are not mindful when sharing our story outside of our Christian community, it can create a disconnect for our listeners. Words we tend to use like "Lord," "salvation," and "grace" can be challenging for people to understand. If the meaning is lost on them because the words are unfamiliar, it's unlikely our story will be heard and understood.

Body Language

- Smile! You have good news to share that can impact their lives. Try putting a smiley face at the top of your notes to remind you to smile.

- Most gestures are good in the context of normal conversation. It is only when a gesture becomes repetitive that it is distracting. Do you overuse the same hand gesture, touch your glasses, or move your hair? These are gestures that have the potential to be distracting. Video yourself or ask a friend to learn if you have these, as they are often unconscious to you.

- Keeping an open posture (not crossing your arms or clasping your hands) puts you and your audience at ease. When in a group setting, point your toes toward your audience. This keeps you engaged with them.

- Align your body language with your verbal message. Your gestures should complement or amplify what you are saying. For example, saying, "This was exciting news!" while slouched over sends a very confusing message. When in doubt, people believe body language.

Technology

- When using PowerPoint, video, or other audiovisual technology, have a backup plan in case it doesn't work. Bring an extra thumb drive with your slides and video. Make sure you have enough cords for your equipment.

- When speaking to a large group, an option is to arrange for an audiovisual person to run the technology so you don't have to focus on it.

- Bring a printed copy of your notes and enough copies of your handouts if using them.

5. Presence: Be Real versus Perfect

Over the years, I have observed that people who are able to share their story from the heart, within their own style, have a greater connection with their listeners than someone who is polished and perfect. Being real versus perfect often leads to building trust.

I believe God planned it this way. He knows who can hear from whom. For example, He knew that people would respond to Moses despite his imperfections.

> "*Moses said to the Lord, 'O Lord, I have never been eloquent, neither in the past nor since You have spoken to Your servant. I am slow of speech and tongue.'*

The Lord said to him, 'Who gave man his mouth? Who makes him deaf or mute? Who gives him sight or makes him blind? Is it not I, the Lord? Now go; I will help you to speak and will teach you what to say.'

But Moses said, 'O Lord, please send someone else to do it'" (Exodus 4:10–13, NIV).

Do you ever feel that way? "O Lord, please send someone else to speak."

This feeling is not uncommon because public speaking, and speaking up in general, is a top fear for most people. Sometimes, we wish to defer to someone else to share the message God has called us to share. We begin to feel unqualified for the task or that we will somehow let God down due to a perceived fault or inadequacy.

You are qualified; you have a unique story, voice, and personality that represent your faith journey in a way that someone needs to hear and that only you can tell.

God knew Moses was the right person to deliver His message. As with Moses, God uses your unique sphere of influence to deliver stories or messages that He knows people will respond to when heard from you.

We each have a personal style that connects with certain people. Embracing and leveraging your unique style is one way to make your story fun for you and those you share it with. Sometimes we compare our style with someone else's and determine that we are less-than or inadequate. Yet it's your willingness to be real, the way God created you to be, that determines your effectiveness, not a perception of perfection.

Kara and Ray

Let me tell you about two people who could not be more different from each other, yet I have seen the power of their differences be the perfect fit for the people with whom God wanted them to share their story.

Kara is a young, vibrant artist who loves the Lord. Her background in theater, along with her ability to share stories of Jesus through song, has allowed her to connect with the next generation in a way they can receive the message of salvation. She performs concerts and plays and gives her testimony in a unique way that young people respond to. Her style is theatrical, yet perfect for those with whom God has called her to share her story.

Ray is a retired engineer, very quiet and unassuming (although his inventions have earned him national recognition). His heart is to make Jesus known to children from poor communities in rural Mississippi. Through a program he started to help teach them robotics after school, he can share his faith story within his style. His style and approach is practical and helps them see how relevant Jesus is to their lives and futures.

God has a place for your unique style, too! Your story delivered in your style is what someone needs to hear for the Holy Spirit to capture his or her heart. Embrace that with expectancy for who God will put on your path.

Time to Share Your Story with Confidence

God has given us all we need to confidently share our stories when we seek His guidance, trust Him with the results, and use the tools He has provided.

You have been given a mission to share His message. If you share your story to the glory of God, He will not only give you the strength, voice, and confidence to do it, He will bless you and others through it as well. Isn't that thrilling?

> *"But those who hope in the Lord will renew*
> *their strength. They will soar on wings like*
> *eagles; they will run and not grow weary, they*
> *will walk and not be faint"* (Isaiah 40: 31, NIV).

Example: Chau's Story: Authenticity through Vulnerability

Chau's journey and her willingness to share her faith boldly offer a vivid illustration of the transformative power of vulnerability and authenticity. Her obedience allowed the Holy Spirit to work through her, touching lives and leaving a lasting impact.

Chau had been asked to speak at an industry conference of her peers. It was a financial planning conference with over 300 financial advisors attending. Because Chau is a top performer in the industry, she was asked to speak on the main stage platform.

Chau felt nervous, as she hadn't spoken on the main stage for a few years, and she wanted to approach this message differently than she had in past presentations. She wanted to provide an inspirational message based on her own authentic story, including her faith journey with God. Given that her audience included people from a variety of backgrounds and faith perspectives, she was unsure of how they would receive it.

Chau had an initial presentation draft but wanted to put the ideas in this chapter into practice as part of her preparation. She chose to set time aside to gain God's perspective. She also was seeking the confidence to share her story with vulnerability and impact. She shared this about her process:

> I knew that I needed to review and revise my
> presentation based on God's answers to the

questions that I needed to ask Him. I dedicated an evening to worship and asked God what He wanted for my audience, this presentation, and me. I asked, listened, and wrote His responses. His prompting was to share authentically—to share through my own story and to be willing to be vulnerable, share the true journey, and use my own story so that people can hear it.

I revised my presentation based on His promptings. My version of the presentation was a financial presentation with little mention of God. God's version, the one I shared, was created by His Spirit in me. When it was completed, I was inspired and in awe. It's a bold statement of faith.

I thought there was no way my compliance department would approve it, but they did. Then, I feared my microphone would be turned off at some point while on stage. That did not happen. With practice and being proactive to calm my nerves, I was able to speak freely and share my testimony authentically in front of this secular audience, and I received a standing ovation at the end. Only God could have made that possible!

Chau's vulnerability allowed God to shift how people in the audience felt about their lives and faith. She knew the Holy Spirit would do the work in each person's heart. She just needed to be willing to share her faith journey with courage and conviction. God was honored, and people were blessed by her obedience. Chau's full presentation is in Chapter 15: *Steps of Courage.*

PART 6

Voices of Faith
Real Stories,
Real Impact

Chapter 13

Encouraging the Next Generation

On Wednesday, February 8, 2023, a handful of students remained in the chapel following a regularly scheduled service at Asbury University in Wilmore, Kentucky. A student decided to openly confess some of his sins to the small group, changing the atmosphere. This evolved into what is now called the Asbury Revival.[14]

The student body president shared that "there's a young army of believers who are rising to claim Christianity, the faith, as their own, as a young generation and as a free generation—that's why people cannot get enough."

As news of the revival spread, it grew from a handful of students to 15,000 people attending per day. The Asbury revival and its ripple effect across the country is one example that demonstrates how this next generation of youth and young adults want to embrace, experience, and express their faith.

Having a 21-year-old daughter, I have observed that this generation communicates through experiences versus information—through relationships, not just data. When we think about it, Jesus is

---

[14] The 2023 Asbury Revival. Wikipedia. Accessed April 9, 2023.

the same. He wants us to experience abundant life through a relationship with Him, not just to know about abundant life.

This generation has valuable stories that represent how Jesus has helped them with achievements, challenges, and other unique life situations that can inspire people, making God's love and grace visible for others to access. Stories that reflect how relevant Jesus is and that His love and grace are available for all generations.

As parents, family, and friends, we have an opportunity to come alongside them, encouraging them to give voice to their faith and to share their unique stories. When we encourage them to share with their authentic voice and within their style, they are able to speak with confidence and transparency in a way that impacts their generation and beyond.

This chapter is dedicated to sharing a few additional ideas for supporting and engaging the next generation to embrace and share their stories. To facilitate that, I'll draw from three examples:

- Ciara's full testimony: You have been introduced to parts of Ciara's story in prior chapters; here, we'll provide her full testimony, followed by a special message from her mom, which shows how God was moving in both their lives to strengthen their faith and trust in him.

- Arika's Facebook post: Social media is a preferred communication option for this generation to share what is happening in their daily lives. Arika shares with her family and friends in a Facebook post how God gave her new eyes for the work she does and how her faith has been strengthened.

- Horizon Christian Academy: this example represents a group of sixth graders (11- and 12-year-olds) that I had the privilege of teaching at our daughter's school. If you are a homeschooler, parent, or grandparent of a young student, this example could provide some ideas to help you prepare them to start thinking about sharing their own story.

These young people have learned that we all have a story and that their voice has value no matter what their age, personality, or background might be. They learned that their story has the capacity to influence change, make God known, and inspire or encourage a friend to have hope.

Ciara's 20-Minute Testimony to a Youth Group

As a recap, Ciara is the 13-year-old who made it through a very difficult season in her life. It was a season of extreme rebellion followed by God's redemption and restoration. Ciara knew God had given her a unique opportunity to provide hope to families impacted by rebellion and unsure of what to do.

She was initially nervous and unsure where to start, what to say, or how to share her testimony so that it connected with people in a way that inspired hope. You have read about her courage and willingness to invest the time and energy to ensure that her story is shared so that her audience (youth and parents) can receive it.

She is allowing me to share the full 20-minute version of her testimony for you to read. I kept the outline titles so you can see her structure elements. We hope it will inspire you to new levels of hope and faith.

Redeemed from Rebellion

Opening

Rebellion impacts everyone! Understanding rebellion is not easy because it's not a reaction to logic. It's ugly for those going through it and for the family members on the sidelines.

Hi! My name is Ciara, and I am 13 years old. Today, I am going to share my own personal journey through rebellion and how God's grace changed everything for me. My hope is that you will be encouraged that God can redeem things in your life the way He has redeemed mine.

Chapter 1: Trigger Events that Led to Rebellion

My story began when I was three years old when my parents separated. This event led us to move out of state a year later. I was confused because I didn't understand much of what was going on. All I knew was my mom, my sister, and I had just moved away from everything familiar—and my dad wasn't around. His absence planted a seed of abandonment. Months went by, and my dad did not see me. Sometimes, he would book a visit only to cancel right before.

The months began to stack up, and it's now been almost a decade since my dad last saw me. He eventually told the court that he was not going to see me growing up, and I could wait to see him until I was an adult. As a result, the seed of abandonment grew and grew. And I began to deal with this pain in very unhealthy ways. Primarily through rebellion. Can anyone else relate?

Rebellion often is not the result of "intent," it's the result of feeling out of control... And I was out of control. Around nine years old was the time in my life when I started to understand the events that had taken place when I was younger. Thoughts like, *I am never going to see my dad again* made me angry and sad. He wasn't in my life, and I didn't know what to do with these emotions.

But my family was there, and I needed someone to be miserable with me, so I focused all my anger on them. It seemed like the easiest way to cope, along with harming myself. I was unwilling to accept the realities about my dad. I lied to myself to the point where I believed my mom made all these things happen, and that she was the cause of my pain.

Not only did I blame my mom, but I also blamed God. If He loved me, why didn't He make my dad want to see me? After all, that was what I had been praying for. Have you ever questioned God's love for you? Have you ever questioned His goodness? I sure have. When my dad continued to not see me, my sadness turned into anger, and then my anger became hate. And I hated God. I blamed Him for my dad's choices.

I became out of control. I developed a rebellious spirit. My home was like World War III! I would follow my mom around yelling at her. Sometimes for hours. This occurred whenever she asked me to do something. I would manipulate to get my own way. Stealing food and lying happened every day! I treated my sister like she was my worst enemy, bullying her constantly.

I felt angry, sad, and alone, yet I wasn't able to put my feelings into words, and I thought nobody would understand. I thought the things I was feeling were wrong and unacceptable. I isolated myself, building huge walls to prevent anyone from hurting me again. At this point, I wasn't living; I was surviving.

Chapter 2: The Process Out of Rebellion: It's Not Linear

All the ways I acted and things I believed changed in the summer of 2020. I went on a trip with my mom, and I never came home. My mom dropped me off at a therapeutic boarding school. She couldn't tell me in advance because I was a runaway risk. I now found myself at a school in the middle of Nowhere-ville, Montana. This life-altering event changed not only my daily living but also my future.

Because I didn't have an appreciation for anyone or anything at home, I was stripped of all my privileges. Everything was controlled and contained at my school. All decisions were made for me because I had proven I could not be trusted. Plus, there were therapy sessions all the time, and I hated therapy. But I kept being my normal rebellious self. I was unwilling to accept anyone's help on how to deal with my pain or work on my behaviors. I got angry at anyone who brought up God. I was unwavering in my patterns that were deeply rooted in me. These behaviors were the only way I thought I could protect myself.

Several months passed, and I seemed to be as stuck as ever! Unbeknownst to me, my family and friends were consistently praying for me. My mom would pray Ezekiel 36:26 over me.

> *"I will give you a new heart, and I will put a new spirit in you. I will take out your stony, stubborn heart and give you a tender, responsive heart"* (Ezekiel 36:26, NLT).

And God knows I needed a soft heart. Meanwhile, it was Christmas time. I was awarded five days at home because I learned to control my behavior—but my heart was still rebellious.

Something amazing happened, though! Even with my hard heart, God used these few days as a turning point for me. It was during this visit that I had a revelation! My dad might not be in the picture, but I still had an amazing mom and sister who loved me.

They were the ones choosing me. But... they also continued to live life without me present. My family had not stopped flourishing just because I was stuck. They showed me pictures of the adventures they had been on—and I wasn't in any of them. I missed out on these memories. That was heart-wrenching for me. I was missing out on so much, and it made me really sad. And my mom and sister were sad, too. They wanted me to be part of the family.

It was then that I decided I was going to do whatever it took to deal with my issues head-on. It was time for me to have a real heart change. It was time for me to surrender my rebellious spirit and choose my mom and sister just like they chose me.

Over the course of the next few months, I worked on a lot of different patterns that had made me a tyrant. I learned five **valuable lessons** that I want to share with you.

- o   First, **being vulnerable is the key**. No matter how much it hurt or how I thought people would react, I learned I had to be honest if I wanted to find a breakthrough. So, I began to share about my hurts from my dad. I shared how angry I was all the time at my family and everyone else. Talking about it became a key component of my freedom.

- o   Second, I had to **take responsibility**. Yes, some of my patterns and ways of thinking sprouted from the pain in my heart, but I was the one who chose to act on it. I began to acknowledge my part, figure out the root of my behaviors, and then consciously work to fix them.

o   Third, I learned to remind myself that dealing with my patterns and pain was **a process**. I didn't always take big steps; most of the time, it was small ones. There were times when I moved backward. Dealing with these heart issues is often a 'one step forward, two steps backward' process. I had to learn that so I wouldn't be disappointed when I moved backward. When I would get disappointed in myself, I would get stuck because I was unable to look past my mistakes and try again. In reality, I was scared to fail. I had to learn it was okay to struggle. And learning to persevere through these failures has contributed to who I am today.

o   Fourth, I needed to learn how to **accept help.** I was around people who had my best interests at heart, but I didn't want to receive input from them. I had to lay my pride down and be coachable.

o   Fifth, this is where **family** comes in. I realized I could not walk this road alone. During this season, my mom was unwilling to accept my behaviors as a part of our family dynamic. She set firm boundaries. Yet, at the same time, she didn't turn her back on me; she was committed to walking through this refining journey with me. My mom was my number one cheerleader. Her love helped point me in the right direction. My family was the reason I stuck it through, even when I wanted to give up. I couldn't wait to see them again. My sister was also my best friend. I absolutely loved reading her letters, and she always pointed me towards God, even though I still rejected Him. I couldn't have done it without their love and support.

With these five lessons, I was able to work my way up the program's levels. But it wasn't smooth sailing... I became so anxious to just get home that I started to rush the process. I had put too much pressure on myself, thinking that if I was perfect, I would get to go home sooner. Eventually, I was overloaded—and I slipped back into every... bad... behavior I had worked to get out of. It seemed as if I was right back where I started. Only a bigger failure this time. I felt deeply and utterly alone. I didn't know what to do with myself. I was without hope…

I had made a commitment at Christmas to do "whatever it took to deal with my issues head-on." Yet, up to this point, I had not allowed God to be part of my journey. But doing it on my own clearly wasn't working. Try as I may, even with the lessons I had learned—I simply did not have **lasting** change. I needed God to save me from myself.

Chapter 3: Redemption: God's Grace

The turning point happened when Jesus showed up for me in a very personal way. One afternoon at my boarding school, I was having some quiet time. I closed my eyes and asked God to speak to me. Right then, I experienced something I never had before. I saw a picture of Jesus sitting next to me. He put His arm around me, and He smiled at me. At that moment, I knew He loved me, and He was going to be there to help me through this. I knew in my heart I needed to surrender my life and receive His help. And that's what I did.

I woke up the next morning, surprised that I didn't feel any different. The following day wasn't any better, and I was frustrated. Why wasn't this God thing working? I thought I was supposed to be better instantly. Then it occurred to me that maybe I hadn't surrendered completely—so I surrendered again. At that moment, it clicked. Every time something isn't working, I'm supposed to surrender and ask God for help. So that's what I began to do. EVERY time. I followed Proverbs 3:5-6

"Trust in the Lord with all your heart and lean not on your own understanding; in all your ways submit to Him, and He will make your paths straight."

I was learning to submit all my wants and desires and align them to His. Every time I prayed, He would supply, but only for what I needed at that moment. You see, because of this, I learned how to be totally dependent on Him. Don't get me wrong, I was still doing a 'one step forward, two steps backward' process. There was a lot of learning. For example, learning how to forgive my dad. This has been challenging, but if God could forgive me for how I've treated my family—then I knew with God's strength I could forgive my dad for abandoning me. God's grace is sufficient.

A specific opportunity God used to help me repair my relationship with my mom was a horse workshop. It was just my mom and me, accompanied by a trainer. It was a three-day experience with a wild horse. Something you might not know about horses is that the human brain and the horse's brain are wired similarly. This gave me the opportunity to learn about myself because the horse would mirror my behaviors and responses to certain situations. It was a complete eye-opener and game-changer in helping me fix unwanted patterns in my life.

As my mom and I put things we were learning into practice, we were able to get resolution in different areas that were hindering our relationship. We connected in a deeper way during our sessions, and this experience is still a regular topic in our conversations today.

I've had a huge transformation. For many months, I tried to change on my own with little result. But I had God's help this time and I knew His presence in my life was helping me in ways

I could never help myself. God has been with me through it all.

God helped me absorb what I learned. I used to be stressed all the time, but now God fills me with peace. I have learned to stay calm even in high-pressure situations. I used to be full of deceit and bitterness, but God has cleansed my heart. I try to always be kind, grateful, honest, and helpful, using God's help and the tools I have learned. I am transformed and redeemed.

Between my horse workshop and asking for God's help, my heart was truly changing and it was undeniable. The light of Jesus was having an effect from the inside out. Others could tell by the way I spoke and carried myself—and they told me so. They were amazed at the inner peace I was experiencing. I still made mistakes, but I had a heart change, and it didn't go unnoticed. It really is a miracle that I was able to have a complete transformation in my life. But hey, Jesus is all about miracles.

Speaking of a miracle, a short time later my mom surprised me and came to the school. When I saw Mom, I started crying and wouldn't let go of her. As she hugged me, I heard the question I had been working so hard for, 'Ciara, are you ready to come home?'

I graduated! I did it! I reached the last level of the program! This was my dream coming true. This moment represented 17 months of long, hard work away from home. It was the happiest moment I'd ever had in my entire life. My struggles, pain, and abusive behaviors no longer ruled over me. This was the final piece to my puzzle.

Closing

But actually, it was only just the beginning of my bright future. I am daily growing my relationship with Jesus. My life is extraordinarily better. And I am excited about what the future holds. I have the best family that supports me the whole way. I have a life worth fighting for.

The fact that I can even say that is truly astounding. Remember, this is coming from a kid who was a bully. I would terrorize my mom and sister. I was a liar and a thief. I would physically hurt myself because I wanted the pain on the outside to match the pain on the inside. I was so broken that I would think about ways to take my life. But now, because of Jesus, I am here sharing my redeeming testimony with you.

I want those of you who hear my story to realize you also have a story people need to hear. God has a plan for the pain in your life—not only to grow your character but to inspire, encourage, and empower other people. You have been given the chance to use your struggles for God's glory. Your story can reach people that I can't. Some stories are big, and some are small, but that doesn't change the fact that each of our stories is powerful. They carry seeds of hope for others.

Just like I believe God is using my story to impart hope.

So, in closing today, I want to challenge you to ask yourself: What will you allow God to do with your story?

Outcome:

After sharing her story with the group, Ciara received this feedback:

- Many of them were in tears, which she felt was a good sign because she knew it was impacting them.
- They admired her courage to share her story with transparency.
- They loved how authentic she was when sharing.
- They liked her eye contact and intentional pausing.
- They told her that her story would impact so many other people.

Ciara now feels equipped to share her story wherever God opens doors for her to do so. I can't wait to hear more from her as her journey unfolds. She is an amazing, bright, and courageous young woman (at only 13 years old)!

As a parent myself, I wondered what Ciara's journey was like from her mother's perspective. I imagine some of you may also be curious. So, I asked Ciara's mom if she would be willing to share a glimpse into that journey with us. She is willing.

Her side of the story represents how God is at work with His redeeming nature not only in our own journey, but for those who are in the journey with us.

Mom's Side of the Story

When I snuggled with my sweet little Ciara those first few years of her life, I had no idea what my angel would unleash on me and our household after her eighth birthday. I just assumed that my angel would always be an angel, so when Ciara started displaying extreme behaviors in the fall of 2017, I figured my consistent parenting would get her back on track in short order. I could not have been more wrong.

My name is Christine, and I have been a single mother of two daughters since they were three and four years old. My girls, Summer and Ciara, are 12 months apart. Single parenting was far from my original plan, but I was determined to play both roles the best I could while knowing God was going to have to fill in the holes. The girls' father chose not to be part of their life in any capacity. Understanding the potentially devastating consequences of not having a father, I began to (and still do) earnestly pray, "God, heal my children as they go and grow." I never wanted my children to get into adulthood and feel like the bottom of their life fell out. I have spent years working through childhood trauma and abandonment issues, and I refused to pass this on to my daughters. So, my prayer stays consistent, "God, please heal them as they go and grow."

Over the course of two and a half years, Ciara's behavior grew worse and worse. She was in complete defiance all the time, and though everything looked great when other people were around, she was wreaking havoc in the privacy of our home. I tried everything—I mean everything—to get her the help she needed and provide tools for her to work through her rage and rebellious spirit. But Ciara is her own person, with her own choices—and she chose to stay in her behaviors. She made a choice. And I did, too. My choice after two and a half years, when she was eleven, was to remove her from our home and send her to a therapeutic boarding school.

Up until this point, keeping Ciara (and Summer) safe was about keeping them close to me. Making the decision to remove Ciara from my home came with much prayer. How was I, her mother, going to be able to send her away? Keeping her safe had always meant keeping her close—until now. Now, keeping her safe was letting her go. Keeping her safe was allowing her to wrestle with herself and God—*somewhere else.*

I had to surrender to the fact that I needed to allow her to go wherever the process was, do whatever it was going to take, however long it was going to take, and be all in with her. And that was my own wrestling with the Lord, allowing her to go away and waiting on His timing.

After dropping Ciara at her therapeutic school 21 hours from home, I felt numb. I drove 50 miles down the highway, pulled over, and slept in my car for four straight hours before waking. I was physically, mentally, and emotionally depleted. When I woke, I heard the Lord clearly speak to me. "I'm answering your prayers for healing as she goes and grows." This awful, abusive behavior by Ciara was ugliness in her heart that needed to come out. I think that, unknowingly, I had an image of God healing her through cuddles, snuggles, hugs, and kisses. But no, this was a tug-of-war between Ciara's will and her spirit. I had to let go and let it be what it was. Ugly. Messy. Exhausting. Lonely. So very, very lonely. I think it's only natural that we form expectations of how God will answer our specific prayers. And my prayers were being answered the opposite of how I wanted the answer to come.

I knew deep down that Ciara was going to have to choose for herself, to let God change her. But what if she didn't choose to surrender? What if she did not choose to allow God to heal her? There I sat, face-to-face with my own fears, having no idea what Ciara would do with this time away. I felt like I was free-falling. But at that moment, I resolved in my heart, regardless of Ciara's choices, that God is good, and I would continue to serve Him. I would serve Him even if Ciara continued to derail.

This resolve sparked in me a renewed hope and energy. I searched for promises in God's word for this season apart. I came upon Ezekiel 36:26: *"I will give you a new heart, and I will put a new spirit in you. I will take out your stony, stubborn heart and give you a tender, responsive heart."* This verse became my faith prayer for 17 months as Ciara was absent.

We reunited as a family at Thanksgiving of 2022. Our family dynamic is back to one of peace and joy. Seeing Ciara embrace the new changes in her life has been a miracle. The fact that she now has a desire and the courage to share her story with others in a way that gives them hope is a blessing I had not anticipated. God is good! He has answered my prayers for Ciara and our family. I want to encourage parents to trust that God will show them what is best for their families.

Arika's Story: Social Media for Kingdom Purposes

Social media has become a preferred communication method for a lot of people! Although there are many opinions about its use, one thing we know for sure is that God can use all things for his purposes, including the stories we share on social media.

Just as we can be intentional with the stories we share in person; we can be intentional with the stories we share via social media. Although there are a few considerations specific to social media; such as keeping our stories short or knowing we can't always know who will be reading it, we can still share how God is working in our daily lives in a way that makes Him more known to our community.

Arika wanted to share with her family and friends how God had given her new eyes for the work she does and how her faith had been strengthened. She decided to share her story with us on a Facebook post.

This example came to me as a member of Arika's family. I was touched by the story she shared and how it reflects that God wants us to experience Him in a personal way, not just an informational way. She gives us an example of how simple it is to share our experiences of God in our daily lives in a way that inspires hope and faith.

Arika's Facebook Post

Hey all! Sorry for the delay. The trip that I took with Life Outreach to Angola last month was incredible and really eye-opening! I have been working with Life Outreach for a year and a half, where my main job is looking through all the footage from their past trips to find the right video to best describe what the hosts are talking about. Since Life Outreach helps support several ministries and nonprofits, I have seen both the need and the need being met. But it is one thing to sit behind my computer looking at these images and another thing to be there and film the stories firsthand. While there are needs being met, there are still plenty of people who do not have anything to eat. Several of the mothers that we talked to hadn't eaten in days, and so, of course, their kids also hadn't had food. Most lost children due to hunger and malnutrition.

There was one story in particular that I can't let go of. One mother described being with her son as he lay dying, hearing his last words and how difficult it was for her. I may not be able to relate to losing a child, but I have lost a parent. Even 17 years later, I still cry on his birthday as I think about all the things I'll never be able to do with him. But the most incredible thing for me was hearing this mother, who had lost multiple children, say that her life was in God's hands. He will provide. She still knows and follows God. If these women, who have almost nothing, can trust in God for everything, then I, too, can also trust God with everything.

So yes, it was an incredible trip!

And happy birthday to my dad, who also helped show me the importance of trusting in God for everything.

The world could use a few more stories like this. If you use social media, consider sharing your experiences with family and friends, showing them how relevant God is to your daily life.

Horizon Christian Academy: 6th Grade Personal Portfolio Presentations

Every year at Horizon Christian Academy (HCA), 6th grade students are assigned a final project that, in effect, summarizes who they have become as a person in their elementary experience. Each student is required to present their portfolio before moving on to Middle School. The project is called *Your Personal Portfolio.*

In this assignment, they are tasked with organizing their personal story to share verbally, along with creating a visual (either a display board, slideshow, or prop) to accompany a ten-minute talk to a panel of adults. As you can imagine, this is quite daunting to the average 11-year-old!

The intention of this assignment is to prepare them to: reflect on what they have learned, organize their thoughts, and share their portfolio information in a clear and concise way.

Because our daughter attended HCA, they asked if I would help prepare these 6th graders by teaching them a few short sessions based on the L.O.V.E. guiding principles.

My hope is that by sharing this example, it will provide you with some ideas and options to help the young people in your life to embrace and share their own story.

The primary approach I took with these students was, "Let's make this fun!" I wanted to take the mystery and fear out of speaking up and sharing their story. The goal was to increase competence and confidence.

The following are a few highlights from each lesson for the L.O.V.E. guiding principles as shared with these students.

Lean on God First

I shifted to **Lean on God First** versus **Listen to God First** as that was easier for this age group to understand. The focus was to lean on God's strength and wisdom. Because…

- He knows you. He created you with a special voice and story that only some people will be able to hear. He wants you to be yourself; He designed you that way. (We discussed the Hebrews Hall of Faith: none were perfect, each was unique, and all were able to be used by God for a purpose).

- He knows your audience. He knows their hearts and minds and what will encourage them from your story.

- When we trust God, he equips and strengthens us for the task.

o Philippians 4:13: "I can do all things through him who gives me strength."

o 1 Peter 5:7: "Cast all your anxiety on him because he cares for you."

o Hebrews 13:5: "Never will I leave you, never will I forsake you."

Organize Your Story

I emphasized that organizing your information into a story is a gift to you and your audience. Using a story structure (open, body, close) is a simple yet effective way to organize your ideas and information, making it easy to follow along and more interesting for your audience.

Following three simple steps and using the story outline template makes this easy to do.

Step 1. Decide what to talk about. A few options to get them started:

- What topic or topics can you share that represent who you are?
- What are your hobbies and/or interests?
- What are you most proud of?
- What event had the most significant impact on your life?
- What has been your favorite class subject and why?
- What have you learned?

We (their teacher and I) also provided the topic prompts below for them to consider. They had already taken the spiritual gifts assessment, so they were aware of their gifts.

Hobbies / Interests	Spiritual Gifts	Character Traits / Talents
Clubs: Awana's, Boy/ Girl Scouts	Encouragement	Leadership
Sports	Leadership	Creative
Music	Mercy	Organized
Theater	Service / Helping	Loyal
Travel	Faith	Inventive / Tech Savvy
Family Activities	Teaching	Sense of Humor
Community Work		Disciplined

Step 2. Using the story outline template, create an outline to organize your ideas into a story. I walked them through how to organize their ideas into open, body, and close, using examples of other students to get them thinking about how to apply it themselves. I kept the elements for each section at a fairly high level. We discussed the following during this session:

- Open:
  - Grab their attention (question, statistic, story, scripture, etc.)
  - Topic Sentence
  - Agenda

- Body:
  - Decide your main topics: two to five topics
  - Tell us about those topics and their impact on you
  - Use visual aids to make it interesting
  - Be clear, and don't rush through the information
- Close:
  - Repeat topic sentence
  - Summary
  - Thank the panel
- Transitions:
  - Transitions are what you say to tie one topic to another
  - Transitions help to reduce filler words (um's, like, totally, etc.)

Step 3. Add in the details that bring your story to life. Once they had their outline, it became easier to add the details. One way to help them consider what details to add was to learn what the panel parents might be interested to know.

Value the Audience

To give the students a way to put themselves in the audience's shoes, and to realize people will be curious about their experiences, I had them do an activity. In this activity the group was broken into smaller groups of 3-4 people. They were asked to each share the topic(s) of their presentation (hobby, sport, travel, etc.) and then the other students asked questions about what they wanted to know about the person and that topic.

Given many students were still not sure what the panel parents might want to know about them, I shared that they would be interested to learn about their experiences in these areas:

- Generally, getting to know you: What are you interested in? What are you most proud of?

- Your experiences at HCA Elementary: What will you remember most about your HCA experience? What was your favorite class/teacher? What is something you learned that will benefit you in Middle School?

- Your faith: What does the word "Christian" mean to you? What will you do with your gifts and talents?

Once the students understood what the audience would be interested in knowing, I encouraged them to integrate some of this information into their presentation. They did not need to answer all of the questions but to use them to help add to their story in a way that helps the audience get to know them better.

In this session, we also discussed how an interesting presentation includes the audience. The more you can bring the audience into your story, the more engaging it will be for them. Some suggestions:

- Ask Questions:
    o Have you ever felt that way?
    o As a student, did you experience…?
    o If you were in this situation, what would you be thinking?
- Use Inclusive Language:
    o Maybe you played a sport in school and also learned…
    o If you have ever played a musical instrument, you may agree…
- Reference their situation or something about them:
    o As parents, you often want to know if your student has…

o   Being part of HCA, you have seen firsthand how the music program has…

Enjoy Sharing Confidently

Nervousness often can come from trying something new and not being sure what it should look like. To help the students learn and have a little fun with this last session, we did an activity.

The class was divided into four groups. Each group was assigned an area and asked to do two skits to represent the topic area they were assigned. First, they are to do a skit showing a "bad" version of that topic and then a "good" version. The four topic areas assigned were:

- Voice: Use words intentionally (too many filler words) and how you say them; speaking clearly, with good pace (not too fast or too slow) and volume (so we can hear you).
- Body Language: Avoid fidgeting, posture (stand straight), body movement (not pacing like a lion or stiff like a statue), and hand gestures (it's okay to have gestures that describe something like swinging the bat).
- Eye Contact and Facial Expressions: Look at the audience more than your visual aid; look at everyone at some point during your presentation, and smile.
- Appearance: Pay attention to your appearance, make sure clothes and hair are neat and clean, no gum, no jingling stuff in pockets.

Ultimately, we wanted them to be themselves but aware of distracting body language that could get in the way of their confidence.

Example Student portfolio presentation using the Story Outline Template

Open

Introduce yourself:
Hi, I am Jordan. I am 12 years old and I have been attending Horizon Christian Academy since preschool.

Grabber (question, story, statistic, scripture):

I would like you to think about the number 33,600. Do you have any idea of what that number means to me? (They respond.) Very good guess! I dive into the water 33,600 times a year! My experience with diving has influenced me to become the person I am today.

Topic Sentence: Three things have shaped who I am and what I enjoy doing.

Agenda: Today I will talk about diving, Girl Scouts, and my HCA experiences.

Body

1st Chapter: Diving

- I started when I was 8 (picture at Palomar).
- I get to do it with my cousin (picture of us doing a synchro dive).
- Types of dives and competitions (describe and show picture)
- I learned: practice and determination helps win dive meets, how to overcome my fears.
- I'm most proud of making it to Nationals and placing 8th place (show medal).

Body: 2nd Chapter: Girl Scouts

- I started Girl Scouts as a "Daisy" at age 6 and over the years moved to "Brownies" and then "Junior Girl Scout."

- I love that my friends and I get to do fun things and earn patches (show some patches).

- We get to help at the Ronald McDonald House and the Food Bank.

- Each year we sell Girl Scout cookies and I learned to set goals, talk to people, manage money, and teamwork.

- Last year, I set a goal to earn a trip to camp and I achieved it, selling 525 boxes. (Share funny story of Dad helping me.)

Body: 3rd Chapter: My HCA Experience

- As a ASB class representative—It has been so fun! We get to decide on theme days at school, like FROG Day and Disney Day. As a class representative, I learned to be more responsible and use my spiritual gifts of leadership and service.

- My favorite class is P.E. (physical education). Coach Randall is fun, and she encouraged me to compete for the "One Minute Club," which is where you hang in a flexed arm hang. I hung the longest at our school—2 min. and 28 sec., beating the school record for girls.

- My favorite project: "The Surf Shack." We had to create a company and I got to use my creativity and math skills. We made smoothies for the entire class.

- Mrs. DeMoll tells the best stories and helped me to learn about God and Jesus during chapel each week.

Close

Summary:

- I have enjoyed sharing with you my HCA experiences, along with how I have grown as a person through Girl Scouts and Diving.

Thank the panel parents: Remember to give them a thank you card.

- Thank you for listening to my presentation. Do you have any questions?

As you have read throughout this chapter, these students and young adults learned that we all have a story and that their voices have value and impact no matter what their age, personality, or background might be.

They learned that their story has the capacity to influence change, make God known, and inspire or encourage a friend to have hope.

It is exciting to think about the impact this next generation is going to have on our future.

Chapter 14

Deliver a Compelling Ministry Partnership Story

Key supporters, donors, and advocates often start as audience members attending an event to hear about the ministry. If you are a ministry spokesperson, your challenge is to capture their hearts and minds so that they want to know more and become involved.

Yet, it's a crowded landscape for nonprofit ministries that are vying for the attention of these potential donors, supporters, and advocates. This crowded landscape can make it hard for your ministry's mission and impact to be heard and acted upon.

If you've ever asked yourself how other ministries can cut through the noise of this crowded landscape to gain supporters, here's how: Deliver a clear, concise, and compelling ministry *partnership* story that connects the hearts and minds of your audience to your cause.

To deliver a compelling partnership story that connects, you will want to address the inherent questions most people have that help them decide their level of participation with your ministry—especially business-minded audience members.

The most common questions that audience members want answered before deciding their level of participation with a ministry:

- What is the focus of your ministry, who do you serve, and why should I care?

- What do you need to accomplish your mission and/or move forward?

- What is your approach and/or model to execute to meet the need?

- How can I make a specific difference with my time, talents, networks, or resources?

- Is there urgency? Do I need to act now?

- How is God working in and through your ministry? Is faith in God being furthered through the ministry's efforts?

Most nonprofit ministry speakers are good at addressing the first question and engaging their listeners' hearts, but not as intentional and clear about addressing the other questions. When a ministry speaker is not mindful of addressing these inherent questions, the following scenarios could result:

Dave, the founder of a discipleship-focused ministry, wanted to expand the ministry's efforts and was looking for support and funding. A local pastor pulled together a group of seven people, men and women that the pastor felt could help this ministry get to the next level.

Here is how an entrepreneur who attended that dinner framed the outcome of the evening with me the next day:

> By the time the evening was over, everyone liked Dave, loved his work, and trusted him. But no one really had a clear idea of what the action items were or what the next steps were. It wasn't clear where or how we could help.

> There we were, all heading off in our separate directions, without a clear idea of what to do. Given that, we all walked away, people who could fund him, people who could guide him, people who could give meaningful support. We all walked away without a clear idea of where to go from there.

Another scenario: The county director for an international ministry held an event in America for approximately 50 people. The global director shared with me how it went:

> The country director did a nice program, with a video of the "Opening of the Gospel" in his country. He then shared what God had done in that country over the last year, followed by having a partner come up to share his enthusiastic testimony about the ministry. He did a good job of celebrating the past and generally talking about the future.
>
> However, when it came time to introduce a special project and the "ask," he thanked the audience and referred them to a document on the table to learn more about the project instead of giving a focused, clear, "Here's what we are all about moving forward, and here's how you can help.

Regretfully, this ministry speaker treated the audience's future support as a separate transaction instead of an integrated part of a compelling partnership story that moves the mission forward.

These speakers represent worthy causes and are passionate people who want to serve God well. Yet they were unable to share a clear and concise picture of what partnership looks like for their ministry.

They may have felt awkward or like they were being "salesy" to ask for support directly, which prevented them from sharing a solid invitation to partner. We sometimes need to be reminded that God uses the body of Christ to fund and support His vision. He is the One that gives provision.

Your audience wants to use their time, talent, network, and resources to make a Kingdom difference. When you show them how to do that, you are offering a gift to your listeners: the opportunity to partner with God's global or specific work. If we miss this part of the message, we miss the impact on THEM as well as your ministry.

The more specific the "ask," the more opportunity for your listeners to feel that their contribution makes a difference. Don't leave them in the dark or confused about what partnership looks like for your ministry.

As author Sam Horn states, *"Confused people do not say yes."* When audience members are unclear or confused about a ministry's mission and/or their role in helping move that mission forward, the tendency is to do nothing.

It's critical for ministry speakers to establish a ministry partnership story that addresses the audience's inherent questions, along with the heartfelt and inspiring stories of the ministry mission in action for those it serves.

Deliver a Compelling Partnership Story

I am a member of a Christian organization called The Barnabas Group (TBG).[15] The organization's mission is to connect

---

[15] The Barnabas Group: San Diego and Orange County groups. www.sandiego. barnabasgroup.org.

marketplace leaders with ministry opportunities, building relationships that allow God's work to flourish.

We meet quarterly, with an average of 400+ attendees in southern California (TBG is a national organization with chapters in many states). At each meeting, there is an inspiring keynote speaker and four nonprofit ministry speakers who share their mission and vision for their specific ministry.

The Barnabas Group audience is composed of successful businessmen and women who want to make a Kingdom difference with what God has put in their hands regarding time, talents, networks, and resources. They attend these meetings because they want to hear about how God is working through these ministries and to learn how they can *specifically* help these ministries reach their next level of impact.

Given that, they want and need each ministry speaker to show them what that support can look like for their specific ministry. At TBG, we believe that the Holy Spirit will prompt the hearts of individual audience members to know when to get involved as they hear these stories.

The biggest gap I observe in ministry presentations in connecting with the audience is that they don't show the audience what partnership looks like and how that impacts ministry progress and outcomes.

The co-founder of The Barnabas Group, Jim West, shares that many Barnabas members (called partners) want and need options to get to know the ministry before jumping in with both feet. Deeper relationships and support often follow once a few "dates" have happened. Jim says, "Most people don't get married on a first date."

We encourage each ministry to integrate stories of its supporters' and volunteers' efforts into the overall story of the ministry's mission and outcomes. We advise speakers not to save what partnership looks like for the end, offering up a list of volunteer items to choose from. Instead, we encourage them to integrate examples of what being a supporter, volunteer, or advocate looks like in action throughout their presentation.

Giving a clear picture of partnership, along with how that support positively impacts those whom the ministry serves, helps listeners understand how they can personally be key contributors to the ministry's next chapter moving forward.

Ultimately, ministry speakers want to find the Sweet Spot of combining God's story, the ministry story, and the audience's story so that there is clarity around how this specific audience can join God in what He is already doing through the ministry.

Young Life: Impacting Hearts

Jay and Shane Panther

The following example is from a ministry organization that presented at a Barnabas group quarterly meeting.

Context: The Panther brothers are bright, passionate, and focused on growing a Young Life ministry that helps kids in foster care. When we started working together, they had a lot of good ideas for this presentation, but they also had a lot of information to draw from and wanted coaching on how to distill it down to meet the audience's needs and within the seventeen-minute timeframe they had been given.

Our coaching followed the L.O.V.E. guiding principles approach. Here is a snapshot of our process together:

Listen: We prayed and sought God's guidance as we began and all along the way.

Organize: Given the amount of information to potentially share, we started with an outline that would give them the "big picture" elements first. Next, they identified key elements to include in the open, body, and close. Here are highlights of what they chose to focus on.

- The opening focused on three things: God's purpose for the ministry, Jay and Shane's unique story for starting the ministry, and why this ministry effort is so important to all of us.

- Body: As they filled in the details to bring the outline to life, they also chose to use one person's story (Joseph) as a thread to demonstrate the mission's process and impact in action. This story helped the audience connect at a human level and stay connected to the heart of the mission along the way. They also connected Joseph's success to the volunteers' contributions along his journey with the ministry.

- Close: They ensured that the audience was clear on how members could participate moving forward.

Value: Once Jay and Shane had a good draft of the presentation, we looked at it through the lens of demonstrating what partnership looks like when the audience chooses to take the next step of involvement. They asked themselves:

- Is it clear how this audience can get involved?

- What examples of being a volunteer or supporter that align with this audience can be shared?

Enjoy: Jay and Shane were going to be delivering this presentation together. We discussed the need to practice, especially the handoffs to each other. They made sure to mark the handoffs in the notes so they could easily transition. Practicing also enabled them to stay on target with key messages yet stay comfortably within the 17-minute timeframe. In the end, with this preparation, they were able to be themselves, have fun, and engage their audience.

Young Life: Impacting Hearts Outline

Story Theme:

Christ-centered, relational-based, mentoring ministry to kids in the foster system. Mission is to introduce every child within the foster care system to Jesus Christ, help them grow in faith, provide them with the sense of family they have been deprived of, and lead them toward self-sustaining adulthood.

Opening:

- God is providing an avenue through Young Life for foster kids in Orange County to learn about Him in a way that changes their lives forever.

- Our unique story: from professional athletes to answering God's call.

- We care because foster kids are targets for sex trafficking, homelessness, and incarceration, which affects all of us. Foster kids need our help. God loves them and calls us to join Him in helping.

- Motivated by love of Christ, we are doing something to enact change.

Body of your story: 1st Chapter:

What Foster Kids Need

- We are a Christ-centered, relational-based, mentoring ministry to kids in the foster care system.
- Work with government agencies to introduce every child in foster care to Jesus Christ.
- Government systems can't do it all. We live in a broken world, outside of what God intended.
- Each kid in foster care is there because they have parents who abused them or neglected them. These kids have lost control, and they have questions.
- Introduce Joseph's story.

Body: 2nd Chapter:

How We Help Them

- Weekly meetings—each component serves an intentional purpose: family style dinner, game, a Bible-based talk, fun.
- Example of each component as experienced by Joseph.
- How volunteers and mentors specifically came alongside Joseph (people like you here tonight).

Body: 3rd Chapter:

Foster Care Challenges Impact All of Us

- Joseph lives ten minutes from here. There are 2500 "Josephs" in *our* backyard.
- Statistics for foster care: human slavery, incarceration, and joblessness.
- When they age out, foster kids are asked, "Do you know one person you can trust?" Most say "no." God is changing that through us.

Body: 4th Chapter:

Together We Can Help Change These Kids' Lives

- Other agencies connect and advocate for us, making Young Life accessible for all foster youth in Orange County.

- Kids need people they can trust. Trust is built through meetings, mentoring, camps. Young Life thrives and moves because of adult volunteers like you.

- Adults like you are ushering kids into the kingdom and changing lives in the process. Example: A volunteer helped Joseph with his resume, drove him to interview, mentored, etc.

Concluding Your Story:

- These kids need you! They live next door to you and their lives are horror stories. You are perfectly equipped to help!

- Ways to partner with us: volunteering, connecting us with your church, come to the event next Saturday—details are...

- We pray a lot for a lot of things, but our biggest prayer is that this ministry is to be put out of business!

Here is the full 17-minute Ministry presentation based on the above outline, as it was delivered to the Barnabas Group Summit meeting.

Young Life: Impacting Hearts

Opening

We are excited to be here today to share with you how God is providing an avenue through Young Life for foster care kids here in Orange

County to learn about Him in a way that changes their lives forever.

People often wonder how two guys like us got involved with this ministry.

We are brothers, eight years apart, and best friends. We were both professional athletes. Sports was the only job we ever had before we started this ministry full-time.

I (Shane) was a soccer player in the MLS with REAL Salt Lake.

I (Jay) was a professional skier with the U.S. Ski Team.

We were both driven, goal-oriented people who knew the value of sacrifice and dedication. We were also both completely self-focused and selfish.

God has lined our stories up in a really cool way. Seven years ago this summer, God dramatically touched both of us and we both, independently of the other, dedicated our lives to God. He has dramatically transformed us, and we both felt called to dedicate ourselves to sharing the transformative love of Jesus Christ with kids. We packed our bags and came to southern California to be with our mom and see what God had in store for us.

At that time, our mom was volunteering with an organization called Hidden Gems. Hidden Gems helps people escape from sex trafficking. We learned through our mom how the sex trafficking industry preys on foster kids and how vulnerable they are due to their circumstances. When she shared this information with Shane and me, we agreed that what is happening to kids in foster care is totally unacceptable!

Being motivated, intelligent people, like all of you, and motivated by the love of Christ, like all of you, we decided to do something to enact change! Young Life: Impacting Hearts was born in Orange County six months later. Seven months later, we opened our first Club in northern Orange County.

Chapter 1: What Foster Kids Need

Young Life: Impacting Hearts is a Christ-centered, relational-based mentoring ministry to kids in the foster system. We work with the Department of Child and Family Services and foster family agencies to introduce every child within the foster care system to Jesus Christ, help them grow in their faith, provide them with the sense of family they have been deprived of, and lead them toward self-sustaining adulthood.

Many of you may be familiar with Young Life, and we are Young Life, but our specific focus is on kids without parents. Young Life is worldwide, but we started this specific brand of Young Life in Los Angeles and have expanded into Orange County. Our Young Life group only focuses on foster youth in LA and Orange

County. Many of us understand how important parents are to a child. How would your life look different if you didn't have a single adult who was consistent and loving?

The foster system is a scary place, not because the system is doing something wrong, but because the system is functioning in a broken world, outside of how God intended parents to care for children. The system only exists because of broken, hurting families. The foster system is a band-aid on a broken leg, doing the best it can and doing an amazing job considering the circumstances. But the circumstances are dire, and the trauma for these kids is staggering.

Every kid in foster care is there because they have parents who abused or neglected them. They went through a horrific separation and lost complete control of their life. The kids have questions… Why don't my parents love or want me? Why won't they change? Who is going to take care of me?!

We see the outworking of this horrific experience every day, but more importantly, we see light in the darkness!

I want to introduce you to our friend, Joseph. Joseph was one of the first kids we ever worked with. Joseph and his sister were taken from their family when he was eight years old. His father went to prison for gang-related activity, and his mother was a drug addict deemed unfit to care for him. Joseph and his sister were separated into different group homes (a group home is a place for foster youth run by staff who rotate out every eight hours). Joseph was really struggling when he showed up at one of our weekly clubs.

Chapter 2: How We Help Them

Club is a separate weekly meeting for middle school, high school, and college-aged youth. Each club consists of a family-style dinner, fun/silly games, and a faith-based message/talk. Each component of the club serves an intentional purpose.

o   The family-style meal creates space to talk. It also allows the kids to serve each other and experience the benefits of service.

o   Every game lets the kids see the leaders act goofy and helps to break down the walls youth have built around themselves.

o   The talk is given by a different leader each week. The message is straight from the Bible, and leaders share how it relates to a part of their own story. This vulnerability shows the kids that Club is a safe place to be honest and allows them to see the leaders in a personal way.

Club also regularly consists of classes teaching independent living skills such as grocery shopping and cooking, how to create a resume or budget, and applying for college or jobs. Many of these youth have never been taught the basic life skills necessary to become self-sustaining adults who contribute to society. We currently have three clubs that reach kids ages 11 to 25, with thirty volunteer leaders engaging sixty kids a week and serving over two hundred unique kids this year.

Our goal is to have nine club locations strategically positioned throughout Orange County. This way, as the youth get transferred from home to home, they are always within close proximity to one of our clubs. The club locations are provided by church and community partners who donate their facilities.

Joseph ended up at Club because one of our volunteers called his group home to tell them about the ministry. The group home staff was excited for a break and decided to drop the kids off with us. Joseph was 16 years old and heavily involved in his neighborhood gang. He was not attending school and was on probation for violence and theft. He was rarely sober and always angry. He had a one-year-old daughter he'd never met.

The first couple of times Joseph came to Club, he didn't speak or smile; he simply sat in the corner scowling, watching, the weight of all his trauma burying him. The leaders diligently said hello and asked him questions, even with no response. Finally, Joseph started speaking a little, offering his name, then a smile, then laughter, which he attempted to hide. Within a couple of months, Joseph was interacting and having fun like a teenager should. Eventually, Joseph shared his story and current life situation.

He admitted that he wanted out of the gang but was scared. With a network of loving, supporting adults providing security, encouraging new friends, and an understanding that God loves him and wants what is best, Joseph started the process of turning his life around.

He decided to leave his gang, knowing there would be consequences. The gang members violently beat Joseph several times before granting him freedom. After each beating, he came to a Young Life leader's house to get cleaned up and, more importantly, loved. Joseph started attending school again and got sober for the first time since he was 10 years old.

Next, he decided he needed a job. An adult volunteer leader, just like you guys in this crowd, helped him to write a resume, offered some basic interviewing training, and then drove him to the interview—Joseph got the job! When Joseph graduated from high school, the world was at his fingertips. Again, an adult volunteer leader helped him apply for college, look into the military, and consider careers. One volunteer had a connection at UPS, and Joseph got a job loading cargo. He took that experience and now has a United States Postal Service career! He has been with the USPS for three years and is in the process of getting custody of his daughter. She is seven years old and has a healthy daddy who loves her and is fighting for her!

I imagine many of you have connections that could help kids get jobs and careers. Please help us grow our database of resources.

Chapter 3: Foster Care Challenges
Impact All of Us

Joseph grew up in Orange County; he lived less than ten minutes from here. There are over 2,500 "Josephs," foster children, living in your neighborhoods, in your backyards, in Orange County right now. The reality of what is happening to these children is simply unacceptable, and we can change it!

Human slavery, which consists mostly of sex trafficking, is the fastest-growing criminal industry in the U.S., and 80% of the people enslaved are currently in the foster system! Young Life: Impacting Hearts has not had a single child fall victim to sex trafficking because kids know they are loved and have value! They are not susceptible to manipulative pimps.

For the average foster youth, within two years of aging out of the system at 18, nearly 70% of the kids are dead, homeless, or in jail, and only 2% ever report having a full-time job. Every youth in our program is working, in school, or both, because they have mentors encouraging positive decisions. None of our youth have ever lived in extended homelessness because they have a support system.

Eighty percent of people incarcerated in the state of California are or were in the foster system! We have not had any youth in major legal trouble in over three years. The average foster youth lives in thirteen different homes before age 18. The transitory nature of the youth makes it very difficult to establish consistent relationships with adults, peers, and support systems. Young Life: Impacting Hearts' kids are becoming sources of joy in their homes and are getting in trouble much less, and therefore, moving much less.

The foster care system is run by tax dollars. Most of these kids end up on federal and state support for the rest of their lives. Honestly, unfortunately, they are a huge drain on the economy. In addition to Jesus' command to care for the orphans, it is practical to help these kids become self-sustaining adults.

As youth age out of the foster system, they are all asked one question during their exit interview, "Do you have one person in your life that you can trust, that you can go to in a time of need?" The vast majority say, "No!"

Chapter 4: Together We Can Help Change These Kids' Lives

God is changing that through us! By all rights, Joseph should have fallen prey to all of the statistics, but he was the outlier, the exception. Furthermore, we have met with the Department of Child and Family Services and foster family agencies (Orange Wood, Olive Crest) and they have expressed the need for Young Life: Impacting Hearts. They are excited to advocate for us.

With these relationships, we can make Young Life: Impacting Hearts accessible to every foster youth in Orange County!

We believe every young person has the right to hear about Jesus in a way they can understand, allowing them to make their own decision about Him. We achieve this by living alongside young people in their worlds and sharing our lives with them—incarnational ministry.

Foster youth need stable, consistent, relational connections with positive parental figures. Young Life: Impacting Hearts creates environments where leaders can establish real, trusting relationships with the kids to offer them the love and family they need. These relationships are formed through weekly youth Clubs, special events, and weeklong or weekend camps.

As natural relationships form, our leaders turn into mentors who can walk through life with the kids daily. We talk about "earning the right to be heard" and know that "kids don't care about how much you know until they know how much you care." We also do fun really, really well! The fun of Club initially captured Joseph and put a glimmer of hope in his eyes. Our fun excellence is so high it's impossible to describe with words, so we want to show you a quick video that only begins to capture the fun energy. (Show one-minute video.)

Some of that video was from our time at camp. Young Life executes the camp experience with the highest level of excellence. It cannot be described, only experienced! Spending 24 hours a day together means seeing each other at the highest and lowest points. This accelerates a trusting relationship in ways that are nearly impossible to experience in day-to-day life. Removing routine distractions and living in a new environment creates an unparalleled opportunity to experience God. Joseph had the time of his life at camp; he still talks about some camp memory every time we hang out. Camp was also his first break from gang life. This summer, we took 25 people to camp; none of them will ever be the same.

Young Life thrives and moves because of adult volunteers who commit their time and energy to help mentor, develop, and invest in the lives of youth. Due to the transitory nature of kids in the foster system, our leaders must be dedicated to pursuing relationships with each child as they change homes, schools, and friends. We ask volunteers to have a minimum of two points of contact each week with the kids. This includes weekly Club, Bible studies, lunch, attending sporting events/activities, or just bringing them along while doing everyday things like laundry and grocery shopping.

Our volunteers are people just like you, adults with careers, families, passions, and schedules! Can you mentor a senior in high school and help them transition into adulthood well?

Some of our current volunteers were kids who were a part of Young Life: Impacting Hearts. We have seen three kids turn into leaders and are now advancing the gospel into the neighborhoods in which they grew up. We also have three former youth training to become volunteer leaders!

As much as we have seen the lives of kids transformed, we are also seeing the leaders transformed in miraculous ways! Our mentor leaders have been involved in everything from high school proms to waiting in court for a verdict on a youth's opportunity to be reunited with their parents. We have leaders who have adopted kids they met at Club, leaders who are currently fostering kids, leaders who have become chaplains at group homes, and who have provided short-term homes for kids in transition.

Adults like you are ushering kids into the Kingdom and having their lives transformed in the process! Finally, we engage our kids in a local church because they need as many sources of family, support, structure, and loving relationships as possible.

These kids need loving adults, they need mom and dad figures, grandma and grandpa figures, aunt and uncle figures. They need single adults to demonstrate their current life state well, they need married couples to model healthy relationships, they need parents to model parenting!

Closing

These kids need you! They live next door to you, and their lives are horror stories. You are perfectly equipped to help. If you are interested in volunteering with us, please do! Are you interested in adopting? Even better!

Would you like to learn more about how to help kids in foster care but do not want to adopt or mentor? We have connections to all kinds of ministries serving foster youth in many ways, and we would love to connect with you. Can you help facilitate job opportunities for foster youth or offer life skills training? They need you!

Do you think your church might want to connect with foster youth ministries? Please connect us so we can join hands, shine light in the darkness, and spread the Kingdom to kids without parents!

We pray a lot for a lot of things, but our biggest prayer is that this ministry would be put out of business! We pray that the Church would stack hands and eradicate the need for foster care. Did you know there are more Christian churches in the U.S. than kids in the foster care system? If every church adopted just one kid, the foster system would be out of business!

We are planning a meeting to share more about how people can get involved on Saturday,

September XX—details are in your handout. Please come if the Spirit moves you. We will be staying after tonight's meeting as well; we welcome the opportunity to address any additional questions you may have.

Thank you.

Recap:

Let's look at how Jay and Shane addressed the audience's inherent questions and clearly communicated how the audience could get involved.

- What is the focus of your ministry, and why should I care?
  - o God is providing an avenue through Young Life for foster kids in Orange County to learn about Him in a way that changes their lives forever.
  - o We care because foster kids are targets for sex trafficking, homelessness, and incarceration, which affects us and our nation. God loves them and calls us to join Him in helping these kids.
- What do you need to accomplish your mission and/or move forward?
  - o Connections, volunteers, resources... Adults willing to be mentors, participate in Club meetings and camps...
- What is your approach and/or model to execute to meet the need?
  - o Establish and run clubs, camps, and other activities where foster kids can have a safe place to go, have

fun, and learn while being mentored by caring Christian adults.

- How can I make a difference with my time, talents, networks, or resources?
  o Become mentors sharing your business and life skills, lead Bible study, make a meal for Club meetings.
- Is there urgency? Do I need to act now?
  o Yes, there are 2,500 kids right here in our neighborhood who need help now.
- How is God working in and through your ministry? Is the Great Commission being furthered through the ministry's efforts?
  o Bible lessons are taught at each meeting, leaders and mentors share personal faith stories and the impact on their lives…
- Fruit of this effort—foster kids stay in school, and some become leaders sharing their faith in their communities.
- Vision for the future: a total of nine club sites in Orange County, California.

Outcomes

As a result of this presentation:

- They received dozens of sign-ups for more information or to volunteer from the audience that day.
- Key contacts were made, which led to a follow-up presentation, resulting in $50,000 in donations.
- They have since grown the ministry to six locations, impacting 300 foster children.

- They have become a model for replicating what they do throughout Young Life, starting ministries to foster/homeless/trafficked/incarcerated youth in 60 cities around the country.

Although your ministry may look very different from Jay and Shane's ministry, that's okay. At the Barnabas Group we have coached a variety of ministries, both local and international, using these same guiding principles. Bottom line: you'll want to consider your ministry story from your audience's viewpoint and ensure that you have addressed the questions they need answered to take the next step of involvement with you.

We can also learn about the donor/supporter audience mindset from Nehemiah's petition to the king for his "ministry mission" to rebuild the city walls of Judah.

Nehemiah's Ministry Mission

Like many ministry leaders, Nehemiah felt called to lead a mission that served the people he cared about. It involved gaining support and resources from others to accomplish his goals. His story is written in the Book of Nehemiah, Chapters 1 through 13, in the Old Testament of the Bible.

In Nehemiah's case, his ministry effort started with a broken heart for the Jewish remnant that survived the exile and were now living in disgrace, and for Jerusalem, the city of their fathers, where the walls had been broken down and the gates burned with fire. He was filled with compassion and a heart to do something about it.

Nehemiah prayed to seek God's favor and hand in this situation.

> *"O Lord, let Your ear be attentive to the prayer*
> *of this Your servant and the prayer of Your*

servants who delight in revering Your name. Give Your servant success today by granting him favor in the presence of this man" (Nehemiah 1:11, NIV).

As the cupbearer for the king, Nehemiah knew it would require the king's approval to leave his position to work on rebuilding the wall and gates, along with resources to accomplish his mission. Although he was afraid, he took a step of faith to share his heart and mission with the king.

> *"I was very much afraid, but I said to the King, 'May the king live forever! Why should my face not look sad when the city where my fathers are buried lies in ruins and its gates have been destroyed by fire?'*
>
> *The king said to me, 'What do you want?'"*

Although this required a bold step on Nehemiah's part, he stated the problem clearly and succinctly.

Donor audiences are asking the same thing: what do you want or need to solve this problem?

Nehemiah prayed:

> *"Then I prayed to the God of heaven, and I answered the king."*

Seeking God's guidance throughout the process gives us the strength to step out of our comfort zone and be aligned with His will.

Nehemiah made his first big "ask":

> *"If it pleases the king and if your servant has found favor in his sight, let him send me to the*

city in Judah where my fathers are buried so that
I can rebuild it."

Nehemiah acknowledged the king's interest and recognized the king now wanted to know more, so he could make an informed decision.

"Then the king, with the queen sitting beside
him, asked me, 'How long will your journey
take, and when will you get back?' It pleased the
king to send me, so I set a time."

Nehemiah knew he needed to have an answer. The typical "I'm not sure" or "I haven't determined that yet" would not have gone well with the king.

Vague answers do not go over well with decision-makers. They like to know you have thought this through.

Nehemiah went on to ask for the items that would make this mission successful.

"I also said to him, 'If it pleases the king, may I
have letters to the governors of Trans-Euphrates,
so that they will provide me safe conduct until
I arrive in Judah? And may I have a letter to
Asaph, keeper of the king's forest, so he will give
me timber to make beams for the gates of the
citadel by the temple and for the city wall and
for the residence I will occupy?'"

One challenge ministries often face is asking for "overhead or maintenance" items that will enable them to sustain working in the ministry, like a residence. If Nehemiah was wise enough to put that in his top three requests, we can learn from him. Business-minded donors know the importance of "sustainability" on any big project. They understand that is part of the equation for reaching success. You may need to go back and read that last paragraph again to notice that Nehemiah didn't ask for gold (the financial currency of the day). Instead, he asked for influence and resources.

> *"And because of the gracious hand of my God*
> *was upon me, the king granted my requests."*

God is always the ultimate provider. He works through the resources of others to make that provision happen. Our role is to listen and be obedient when God provides an avenue to make our ministry and its needs known to others.

Here's the wonderful thing about God and His provision: He exceeds even our wildest dreams in terms of what can be provided. Look at what the king did to exceed Nehemiah's requests:

> *"So I went to the governors of Trans-Euphrates*
> *and gave them the king's letters. The king had*
> *also sent army officers and cavalry with me."*

Wow! God provided cavalry and army officers to ensure that Nehemiah could safely get where he needed to go and complete the ministry mission God had placed on his heart.

I believe God wants to provide for your ministry mission as well!

Example: Teen Challenge Ministry

The San Diego Teen Challenge Ministry Director, Mike Conway, was asked to share about the ministry with The Barnabas Group. This example represents three minutes of his seventeen-minute presentation where he invites the audience to become part of a miracle, while making them aware of Teen Challenge's mission and how that makes a difference for those they serve. He used some audience participation and personalization to engage along the way.

Grab a Corner and Be Part of a Miracle

Do you want to be part of a miracle?

Remember the story of the paralytic that no one could help? It's in Matthew 9. There is a paralyzed guy. Day after day, they walk by him. They walk by him his whole life. He's sitting on a mat. What are they able to do to help him?

Let me hear you say "survive." (Audience responds) "Survive!" If we're just treating and surviving and keeping people in depravity, we might say, "Oh well, here, take this and just get through until tomorrow."

We can't just survive. We can't just treat. We need to transform. The Bible verse that we base our whole ministry on, 2 Corinthians 5:17, states, *"If anyone is in Christ, he's a new creation."* God says, "Don't fix him; let Me resurrect him! If anyone is in Christ, he's a new creation. The old is gone. Behold that which is new."

So, here's a paralytic. He's never going to get help on his own. He's never going to get off that corner. He's never going to change. He could promise; he could hope. But one day, Jesus is coming to town, and four people said, "Oh, if we could only get him to Jesus."

You know what they did? They had a vision. They had a *why*. They each grabbed a corner of the mat, four different people. They carried this paralytic, four people, and they brought him to Jesus. And do you know what happened? They couldn't get in the room— there were too many Barnabas people there!

They're like, "Oh no, another obstacle!" But when you have a vision, the obstacles are not going to stop you when you believe that if you can just get that broken, wounded, addicted man, woman, gang member, prostitute, homeless, if you can just get them to Jesus. They each grab a corner and say, "We can't stop!" What do they do? They bust a hole in the ceiling and lower the man down, and Jesus sees their faith.

That's what we are here talking about today; grab a corner. Teen Challenge can't do it alone. I invite you to help grab a corner and become part of a miracle.

The government has studied thousands of our graduates, and they have found that even though there's no cost to come, after completing our one-year discipleship ministry, five years later, 87% of those people are still completely free. Why? Because we didn't treat the behavior. We didn't treat the symptoms. We gave them Jesus, the gospel of Jesus Christ. There's power in the blood to set the addicted free.

Do you want to change your life today? I'm just asking you to grab a corner. Here's what those corners can look like for you...

Chapter 15

Steps of Courage: Stories Shared

This chapter provides the opportunity to read the full testimonies of Laura, Chau, Richard, and myself. Laura provides a five-minute story, while Chau, Richard, and I offer longer versions, between twenty and thirty minutes, that were shared with larger groups.

As you read our testimonies, consider seeking the Holy Spirit's guidance to help you understand what could be applicable to your story preparation given your style, listeners, and situation, or for you personally.

For each testimony, consider asking:

- Father, how are You drawing me closer to You through this example of a testimony?
- Father, how do You see me applying the ideas, principles, or style represented?
- Father, how is their situation similar or different to mine?
- Father, what part of this example would my audience relate to?

Although there is much to be learned, gained, or reinforced by reading these testimonies, I also believe God intends for them to encourage and inspire you to draw closer to Him.

Laura's Five-Minute Testimony

As you read in Chapter 2, Laura had wanted to be able to share her testimony in five minutes versus the forty-five minutes it had been taking to share it. Here is the five-minute version she shared in a small group setting.

A Birthday to Celebrate!

Hey, I have a big birthday coming up this year!

Twenty-one years ago, I accepted the forgiveness of God, and I became His child. Twenty-one years ago, I started my life as His.

I had been in church all my life, but that was the day someone opened the Bible and explained to me who Jesus Christ is and what He was doing on the cross.

I heard Peter 2:24 for the first time that day: "*He Himself took our sins in His body on the tree.*" I heard that, and I got it. Something in me jumped up. I got what He was doing there! It was *because* of me—because of my sin.

The verse goes on to say, "*by His wounds you are healed.*" So it was *because* of me. But it was also *for* me. I was being offered healing. Forgiveness.

And you know what I did? I grabbed for them. I apologized to God for what I did to Him. And I thanked Him for what He did for me. I asked Him to forgive me, to heal me, and join my life to His life. And that day, He did. I stepped from death to life, like the Bible says.

That was the day I saw Him for who He really is. And in light of who He is, I saw *myself* for who I really am.

That day, a *sinner* met her *Savior*. What a relief it was to admit that I am a sinner. It's something we all know, don't we? We just don't want to admit it. But as soon as I did, as soon as I confessed my sin, He took it from me. I was free.

- Do you know Him for who He really is?
- Do you know yourself for who you really are?

What came before that day in my life? Well, a decade earlier, I was in a psychiatric hospital. I have been wrecked by my childhood. I was curled up in that hospital and not eating. I was curled up and not speaking. I was curled up against the pain of this world.

My family looked just right. My father was a Yale-educated doctor; my mother was a musician. We lived in a beautiful area with private schools and church every Sunday. But my parents were not able to be there for each other or for their four children. They divorced early on, and my mother committed suicide when I was nine. Our family was broken up, and by the time I started high school, I had lived in ten different households.

For as far back as I can remember, I was afraid and overwhelmed by the demands life was making of me.

- Do you feel that way some-times?

I became manipulative and angry. By the time I was 20, my life was entirely ruled by fear and self-pity. And I hated myself.

- Do you ever feel that way?

So when this word came to me that I am loved by God, that He knows all about me and my past, and that He offers full forgiveness—this was the word of life to me! And I grabbed it!

- Have you ever grabbed it for yourself?

For 21 years, I have been living as a loved one of God. I am forgiven. I am secure. Life hurts me sometimes. Memories hurt me sometimes. But I am not alone. I am His. And I am at rest. I am fully known and fully loved. I am grateful.

Sin carries us away from God. But I want to tell you that the One who created you wants you back. He is calling you. He is holding out full forgiveness and a new life as His. Only turn in His direction, and He will run to you like the father of the prodigal son did. Turn to Him. Accept the gift of forgiveness He is holding out for you. It is only a prayer away.

Chau's Industry Conference Testimony

Below is Chau's 30-minute presentation, minus a few industry-specific parts that are inappropriate to disclose outside the event. I've also kept chapter subtitles to indicate the turning points in her story.

For some additional context, the primary technology these financial advisors use with their clients is called a *Living Balance Sheet*. These advisors also use a *Scorecard* to track their own performance and their productivity within the industry. For this presentation, Chau wanted to use these two recognized industry tools to shift her audience's perspective on the meaning of success and faith.

Living Your Balance Sheet

I want to share the story of how I climbed my way to the top of this success ladder, how I completely lost myself and became a walking dead person, and how I woke up to my life to find myself on top of a mountain in Costa Rica in 2016. I'll share the lessons I learned along the way and how I'm using what I learned to make a lasting and meaningful impact on my clients' lives.

Five years ago, I didn't have a clue how to answer a few simple questions, like: *What is your definition of success? Where does your definition come from? Who is influencing your definition of success?*

The reality was I was too busy doing, chasing, fighting, and pretending to even think of these questions, much less ask them of myself. Although I asked some of my clients, I didn't really listen for the things that truly mattered in their answers. Instead, I just listened for the things they wanted to do. I've since learned that the real answers to these questions matter a lot.

You have a standard of success, yet have you stopped to examine where it came from?

Whose voice you value determines your definition and measure of success. *Success has a price and a cost. Price* you can define and quantify. *Cost* equals the price plus all the unintended consequences that can't be defined or quantified today but can completely devastate a plan and a life. We teach our clients this distinction as it relates to their money. Yet, don't apply this fundamental truth to all the other life choices. *Cost* is about tradeoffs and living the consequences of your choices.

My Life Before

This is how I defined and measured success five years ago: Club credits, VIP reports, and ribbons. I can look back now and have compassion for myself. Of course, this is how I measured success when my career started with such great uncertainty. I started my practice twenty-two years ago, straight out of college at the age of 21. No warm market, no mentors—just trade shows, street fairs, and the dreaded "All Day Call Day." I was in survival and fight mode.

I left my parents' house when I was 16 with a promise to myself that I would never return to that emotionally, physically, and psychologically violent house again. Thus, I didn't have any parents to fall back on. I had a lot to prove to myself, my parents, my prospects, my customers, my colleagues, and my competitors.

I was driven to prove that I belonged. Fear was my motivator.

I was focused on achieving and succeeding at any cost according to industry standards. Based on production history, I was successful. I qualified for a Top Producer Club for all 18 years of my career. In 2014, I qualified for the President's Council. I'd made it to the top.

I paid a great price along the way. I worked ten hours a day, six to seven days a week. I thought and obsessed about work when I wasn't working. I averaged five hours of sleep per night and ate one large meal late at night on a regular basis. I didn't exercise. I had terrible back pain and didn't make time to get treated. I was in a loveless marriage that was deteriorating more rapidly than I was even aware of.

I was a driven woman! Success at all costs.

I learned a significant difference between *being driven* and *being ambitious*. Being *driven* is to pursue and chase a result at all costs. It's analogous to a police officer chasing a criminal to get him off the streets to keep citizens safe. But in his pursuit, he doesn't notice the mom and son he ran over with his car, the grandmother he shot with his stray bullets or the group of children who had to jump out of his way as he shot past them. He is focused on getting the criminal off the streets at all costs—good intentions with high costs and high casualties.

Alternatively, being *ambitious* is to be clear about the desired result while considering all costs: the short-, mid-, and long-term ripple effects on oneself and others. Take an honest look at yourself. *Are you driven or ambitious?*

I wonder if there is someone here who is waiting for the applause of the wrong person, the wrong people, like I was five years ago. Some of us are doing things and living life to impress people who aren't even paying attention.

Sometimes we get so addicted to the approval of others that *we can't receive the approval from God and ourselves.* That was the woman I was five years ago.

There are moments in your life that make you and set the course for who you're going to be. Sometimes, they're little subtle moments. Sometimes, they're big moments you never saw coming. No one asked for their life to change but it does. It's what you do afterward that counts. *That's when you find out who you are.* "

Life Unraveled

In a span of three years, my life completely unraveled. Beginning in 2013, I experienced my first client death. Wayne was 37 years old and died of a heart attack without having any adverse medical history. His daughter Nicole was four, and his son Dante was two. His wife, Kristine, worked part-time.

On the Saturday morning when I got the call, I raced to my computer to pull up their Living Balance Sheet. I knew Kristine, Nicole, and Dante would have to live with the planning we'd completed when Wayne was alive. They would live with the consequences of their choices, which I had helped them make.

In 2014, my dad had a stroke at 59, which left him completely paralyzed on the entire left side of his body. At that point, he became my dependent. My dad was a laborer, working minimum wage jobs. He didn't even have $100 to his name. He'd been a chain smoker since the age of 14 and only drank Coca-Cola, never water. He only ate things from a box or a can, never fresh fruits or vegetables.

Since then, he's been in a nursing home, and I pay for his care. At 65, my dad is confined to a wheelchair and wears diapers. He and I are living the consequences of his choices.

In 2015, I completed a second failed in vitro-fertilization (IVF) trying to get pregnant, which took a physical toll on my body and an emotional toll on me, only to learn a week later that my husband of almost ten years had been having affairs for the last five years of our marriage. The fourteen years of life we spent together felt like a big lie. I didn't know what was real. How could I have been so blind, so stupid? How could I ever trust anyone again? How could I ever trust myself again? I was 39.

How could I get my fertile childbearing years back? The reality of the consequences of my choices became unavoidably real.

Power of Prayer: God Becomes Real

That's when I learned that "prayer is not a spare wheel that you pull out when in trouble but a steering wheel that directs the right path throughout life." My divorce was a hurricane that completely leveled and cleared what the previous three storms—a client's death, Dad's stroke, and two failed IVFs—left behind.

It brought me to my knees in full surrender to God. I was a cosmetic Christian up to that point, doing and saying what it appeared a good Christian would say and do. God was not in my heart.

How many of us are doing, saying, and engaging in things because it looks good? It seems like what you should be doing is "fake it till you make it." That inauthenticity and incongruence subtly—day by day, act by act—erodes your confidence and your soul, ultimately stealing your joy.

In complete brokenness, I was finally able to receive God's love, grace, and mercy.

I prayed, *God, help me not waste this pain. Show me how to make something beautiful out of this pain. What do You want me to do with my life, God?* That was the beginning of my awakening to my life and journey back to myself and into God's arms.

Storms: The Transformation Journey

Once the storm is over, you won't remember how you made it through or managed to survive. You won't even be sure whether the storm is really over. But one thing is certain: when you come out of a storm, you won't be the same person who walked in. And that's what the storm is all about.

Wayne's death was a valuable gift to me. I experienced the real value of our work in the lives of real people. My dad's stroke was a gift to me because, prior to his stroke, we only spoke briefly on the phone a few times a year. Since his stroke, I visit his nursing home every weekend. I get to practice my Vietnamese. He hasn't had a cigarette, drank a Coca-Cola, or even eaten any junk food since he was admitted into the ER after his stroke six years ago.

Divorce = A New Scorecard

My divorce was the best and truest blessing because it stopped me in my tracks. It gave me an opportunity to take a close look at myself and the woman I'd become. I realized I didn't know her. I didn't like her. I learned that I could let the storms break me, or I could embrace their cleansing power to create a new path. And in the new, clear space, I could choose the woman I want to be.

Because… It's never too late to be what you might have been.

A week after I kicked my ex-husband out and filed for divorce, I was reeling in anger and grief. I told a good friend, "'F' him, I'm going to grow my business, make more money, and move to the beach." My friend smiled and lovingly said, "I'm sure you can do all those things and even more. But you have a great opportunity right now to take a close look at your scorecard."

What are you keeping score of? What are you giving yourself points for? If you die tomorrow, will the things on your scorecard matter? Heck, you could even throw the scorecard away. (What? He's crazy. I track everything!)

You know, my friend was right. None of the things on my scorecard really mattered. I'd been numb and asleep in my life for so long, I didn't know what mattered.

Time Off to Reflect

I took the last four months of 2015 off and traveled all over the country. I stayed with friends and clients who became friends. A few days here, a couple of weeks there. People opened their homes and their hearts to me. *I learned the power of vulnerability,* how to feel, accept my brokenness, and ask for help. And in return, I got true connections and loving friendships. The most important friendship I gained was with myself. I forgave myself. I invested in myself. I learned to love and have compassion for myself. *I turned to God and asked better questions.*

God, how do I live a fruitful life? God,
how do I honor You in all I am and all I do?

I prayed for the answers. Then, I listened and obeyed. Here's what I heard: "Your greatness is not in what you have, it's in what you give."

Life After Pursuing God/Quality Relationships

I stopped focusing on my own pain. I started to see and have compassion for the pain of others. I began to give the most important thing I have: my time and presence. I gave of myself.

Starting in 2016, I began to work eight focused months *so that I could serve* and travel for four months out of the year. I went on mission trips to Costa Rica, Belize, and Peru. I now mentor high school and college students, volunteer with three nonprofits, and coach an after-school running and self-empowerment program for preteen girls. None of these things were in my heart prior to my divorce. The storm cleared the debris of my life, allowing me to *define success with my heart, not just my head.* God became my influencer.

From Vietnam to America

When I closely examined my definition of success and who and where it came from, I realized I'd become my parents. As a child, I witnessed violent fights between my parents, usually about money. We came to America as refugees after the Vietnam War. My parents were in fear and survival mode when they arrived in San Diego with nothing. They divorced, and my mom remarried.

From nothing, my mom and stepdad built businesses, acquired real estate, and grew their net worth. On the outside, it appeared like we were living the American dream. As a child, I personally experienced what money can give you: larger houses, nicer cars, and better neighborhoods. I also experienced what money takes away from you when you're not clear about your true purpose for money and what success looks and feels like to you. Their fights were violent, often involving police officers coming to our house to stop them from seriously harming each other or us kids. In between fights, they'd say, 'When we have more money, we'll be happy.'

I use my pain and hard-learned lessons to help my clients to stop and closely look at their lives, to define their true purpose for money and their personal definition of success. Not what their friends, family, neighbors, or society say is success. Because, like my parents, my clients are experts at making money. *But without knowing your true purpose for money, you'll never have enough.*

As Oprah said, "Be thankful for what you have. You'll end up with more. If you concentrate on what you don't have, you'll never have enough."

Our Work Is Like Chess—Helping Our Clients And Ourselves

Financial organization without clear purpose and a clearly defined win is like playing the game of chess without knowing that to win is to be the first to say checkmate. Without defining checkmate as success, you're just moving the pieces around the game board. You're not playing chess until you know your personal checkmate and how it looks and feels. You will collect financial pieces and products inside the pretense of 'more is better.' You'll focus on growing the numbers on the page.

We teach our clients to play financial chess with our analysis, planning, and strategies. We teach them how money works with our calculators and illustrations. But we don't teach them the important distinction between being rich and being wealthy.

To be rich is to be able to buy things with money. To be wealthy is to be able to buy things and enjoy the things that money cannot buy: health, love, a true sense of security, and peace of mind.

Thus, we can make a meaningful and lasting impact in our clients' lives by helping them to be wealthy and to connect their life's work, i.e., their net worth, with the people and the causes that really matter to them. We can make a meaningful and lasting impact in our clients' lives by helping them to define their checkmate.

We do this by slowing our clients down and having heart-to-heart conversations in which we ask them questions that they don't know or don't want to ask of themselves. We take them beyond the to-do list by asking questions and listening for the answers that go beyond the to-do-and-have answers. We capture their real answers in *their Living Balance Sheet's Goals and Concerns section* so they can keep their personal checkmate fully present.

For them and us, in every meeting, we need to ask questions that help them reflect on their lives. *How did you become who you are today? For whom and what are you growing and protecting your assets? What does a good life look and feel like to you? Tell me more about that. Help me to understand you. How do you want to be known, and what do you want to be known and remembered for?*

We make a lasting impact on our clients' lives by helping them to build a solid financial foundation. Once they know that they and their family are financially safe, we can help them to think and look beyond themselves to the causes they care about, to think about the impact they want to make with their money, their time, and their presence—and to be the change they want to see in the world.

The reality is, you can only ask your clients these questions once you answer them for yourself. You can't lead others where you have not gone yourself.

So what's your win? Your checkmate? Who and what are you playing for? But don't get attached to your identity and possessions. Because at the end of the game, the king and the pawn go back into the same box.

One day, your heart will stop beating, and none of your fears will matter. What will matter is how you lived. This is why I now track time. Time is something we can never get back once we spend it. Time is my scorecard. *What am I doing with the time God has given me?* How can I make a difference in the lives of those I encounter today?

You want to enjoy your life more. You want to create a lasting legacy. *Reflect on your own life storms. All the storms God got you through.*

As you reflect, ask yourself, what did I learn about myself? How can I use my pain for good? How am I stewarding the people I've been given? How am I helping them to be good stewards of what they've been given? Make time to listen for the answers, then obey.

That is your legacy. When you leave this earth, how many lives will have you touched?

Moments of Wealth

Enjoy the little things in life, for one day you'll look back and realize they were the big things. Develop and master the skill of noticing, appreciating, acknowledging, and celebrating *moments of wealth.*

How do you *notice*? By being fully present. How do you *appreciate*? By saying thank you. How do you *acknowledge*? By specifying what you're thankful for and how it makes a difference for you. How do you *celebrate*? By enjoying the experience exactly as it is.

What's a moment of wealth? An experience that no amount of money can make better.

A moment of wealth is watching your child take his or her first step. It's walking hand in hand with your spouse. It's having a friend call out of the blue to tell you they miss you and are thinking about you. A hot cup of coffee or tea on your comfy sofa on a cold, rainy morning. Right now, this is the moment of wealth for me. Our lives are full of small and big moments of wealth.

If we only focus on where we're going, all of our to-do's, and what we still don't have or haven't done, we'll miss our moments of wealth. And that would be so tragic because our moments of wealth give us our life.

So how can you experience more moments of wealth? Grow a grateful heart and mind. A gratitude mindset has significant transformational power in you and how you experience the world around you. Five years ago, I saw the world as a glass half empty. I looked for what was missing; what was wrong. What's not enough? I was blind to my moments of wealth. *Is this how you see the world?*

Joy, like wealth, is not something that happens to you. You must intentionally choose it, regardless of your circumstances. Choose to appreciate and value all you have. Choose to notice beauty and wealth all around you. Choose to make today special because it's the one you have now.

Choose joy. Don't wait for things to get easier, simpler, better. Life will always be complicated. Learn to be happy right now. Otherwise, you'll run out of time.

Choose to notice, appreciate, acknowledge, and celebrate your *Moments of Wealth*. Choose to live out loud. Choose joy as your definition of success.

This is how you live your balance sheet.

Thank you.

Mary Ann's 20-minute Testimony at Church Women's Event

This is my personal testimony that represents the outline you viewed in Chapter 5: *Outline Your Story Elements*. I initially shared it at my own church but have also had the opportunity to share it at a few different women's events. The attendees at these events represented women of all ages who were either members of the church or organization or invited guests. The audience ranged from 30 to 100+ people.

Living Out God's Truth

Opening

Have you ever thought about the statistics in your life and how we let those statistics or culture's view of them define us?

Today, I want to share some of my statistics and how God used them to demonstrate His love, truth, and grace in my life. He can do that for you, too.

The first statistic I want to share is...

5—I am the oldest of five siblings.

17—Our family moved 17 times by the time I was 21. My parents were the original "House Flippers!"

1984—The year I entered my training and development career as part of the Macintosh launch team for Apple Computer. It was an amazing time in history, and that's when I first learned the value of a clear message.

26—The number of countries the Lord has blessed me to visit with my work.

I have certainly been blessed with my career, and I think with these statistics, most people would say my life is pretty good by culture's standards. I have a solid family, a career, travel, and adventure. Some would even say it's "Facebook/Instagram-worthy."

Today, I want to focus on a season in my life where I had a significant shift in my faith that demonstrates how God views our statistics *very differently* than we do.

Chapter 1

The first statistic for this season is *one in a million*. I felt like I had a one-in-a-million chance of getting married at the age of 40. I was single and living in Dallas. And did you know that in Dallas, there are three women to every single man? That didn't help!

I just wanted to meet a nice man and have a family. That was the desire of my heart.

I felt this statistic was pushing against me. It may not be a real statistic, but I think those of us who are single and over 40 would agree—it certainly feels real. And I felt it. I was praying to the Lord, *"Why is it so hard?"* And *"Lord, why can't this happen for me? Am I asking too much?"*

As I prayed, the Lord brought to my mind Psalm 37:4 (ESV): *"Delight yourself in the Lord, and He will give you the desires of your heart."* God wanted me to delight myself in Him first and let Him take care of the rest. He showed me that I had taken my focus off Him and what is truly important to finding fulfillment. With that, He also gave me two things to think about and work on.

The first was, "Look for the right man." He gave me the criteria for the kind of man I needed to be looking for. But the second was more significant: God said, "You need to become the woman that *that man will want to marry because today, he would not want to marry you.*" God was making me aware of the hypocrisy in my own life.

I knew God was right and that if I turned this desire over to Him and trusted Him, He would help me become more consistent with living my Christian values and a life of purpose. I knew He would also help me to meet the right person if it was His will. So, I began to spend time in His Word. I began to spend more time with the Lord in prayer. I also got serious about using the criteria that He had put on my mind when dating.

Are you curious about the criteria?

There are five of them, and I call them the five C's. The first is **Christian**. The Lord wanted me to seek a man who loved Him and lived his life based on that value. I also needed to *be* a woman who lived my Christian values. God wanted us to be equally yoked because that would create a firm foundation for our marriage.

The second is **Compatible**. Compatibility here is different from our culture's view of compatibility. I used to focus mostly on surface things, like: "Oh, you like to waterski? Me too!" "Oh, you like to travel? Me too!" Those are nice, but they're not what the Bible tells us is important. God's Word tells us to get to the values level and be compatible regarding faith, family, friendship, and finances. We need to be compatible with and demonstrate these things in our lives. I must admit, I hadn't focused much on this in my dating life.

One reason is this third C, **Communication**. Even though I'm a communication specialist by trade, I did not have good communication skills when talking about deep issues and important things in life, especially with men. So it's interesting how the Lord, in His wisdom, helped me along with this. While dating, He introduced me to a man who lived 2000 miles away. You get to a much deeper communication level when your dates are a three-hour phone call every Friday night. It helps you to learn if you are truly compatible at the values level.

The fourth C was **Commitment**. I'd had some rocky relationships in my past, and I felt commitment was not valued. I wanted to meet a man who was committed to our relationship but also to the Lord because I felt that if he didn't want to break the Lord's heart, he probably wouldn't break mine. It takes God and commitment to make it through difficult times in life.

Lastly is **Chemistry**. I know we're not supposed to get physical before marriage, but "You've got to like to kiss the guy!" So, the Lord showed me through the *Song of Solomon* in the Bible that it's okay to have chemistry. God planned it that way.

It took another year for me to get committed to doing things God's way. Using these criteria also enabled me to recognize God's choice for me versus what I may have chosen on my own.

As you heard, God put a man who lived 2000 miles away in my life. I knew it was God's hand, given that I met Donnie on a blind date set up by his mom (That's novel in itself!). Then, during our dating, Donnie was put on a special project in Dallas that allowed us to see each other in person. Given that in 25 years at his company, he had never been assigned to a project out of San Diego, we knew it was God's hand. We were married a year later. I felt so blessed that Donnie not only met the five C's but also exceeded them.

I knew the Lord was saying to me, "I don't care what the statistic is. You might feel like *one in a million* to get married after age 40, but I have the power to give you the desires of your heart. Trust me."

Chapter 2

As you can imagine, we came into this marriage with another statistic working against us: **2%**. There is only a 2% chance for a couple to get pregnant after 40 without in-vitro fertilization. At this point, I was 43.

We felt all the pressure! We felt the clock ticking. People said, "Try in-vitro fertilization; that'll be the easiest way, given your age." We began researching and did a couple of tests. All the information being thrown at us was overwhelming.

Then, one morning, Donnie looked at me and said, "You know, I don't feel God in this as I'm praying about it. I don't feel this is the direction God wants us to take."

And I said, "You know, I don't either." We continued to pray about it, but we didn't feel God's hand in in-vitro for us. We decided not to pursue the infertility route any longer. We trusted God had a plan for us.

We turned our focus to looking into adoption and foster care. We had some wonderful people in our church who were already foster parents and involved in adoptions, and they were starting to share with us what we could do. We started to fill out the foster care information... and a couple of weeks later, I was pregnant! We couldn't believe it.

Again, the Lord said, "It doesn't matter what the statistics are; it might be 2%, it might be 1%. I have the power to give you the desires of your heart." In this case, we were blessed with our own baby. Our daughter Jordan was born when I was 45 with no complications.

Chapter 3

Now, it would be nice if my story stopped here...

But if it did, I would be falling short of sharing with you the real transforming miracle that happened for me—the kind of miracle that reveals God's character and how much God loves us. This is the point at which I felt God's grace at my core.

Getting married and having Jordan were huge blessings, but the real transforming miracle for me was what God did for Donnie and me while we were dating.

Have you ever done something in your past that you hold against yourself? A mistake or bad choice where you felt you could not be forgiven?

I have spent a great deal of time—years—feeling that way. It has impacted my faith and my relationships.

The reason is this statistic: **45 million**.

At the time that Donnie and I were dating, according to the CDC (Center for Disease Control), 45 million people had herpes, and I am one of them.

While we were dating, all I could think about was, "I have finally met the love of my life, and now I need to tell him *this*!" Anticipating the conversation brought back the awful, gut-wrenching fear and shame that I experienced when I first learned the news for myself. Yet, I knew I needed to tell Donnie; it was the right thing to do.

I got on my knees and prayed to the Lord asking for His guidance and strength for this conversation. As I prayed, God calmed my heart and brought to my mind Psalm 103:10:

"He does not treat us as our sins deserve or repay us according to our iniquities." It is worth

repeating, *"He does not treat us as our sins deserve or repay us according to our iniquities."*

Through this Scripture, God showed me that He does not treat us as our sins deserve. He wanted me to be reminded that because Jesus had already paid the price for my sins when I accepted Him as my savior, it changed everything. My identity was now in Him, not in what others may think of me. *My veil of shame and guilt was taken away when I became His.*

Once I fully embraced that, accepting His grace, my attitude changed. I now had the courage to face Donnie and tell him. I asked him to take a walk on the beach, where I shared my little secret with him. And... he pulled away. Like other men in my life, he responded with disappointment.

I was hurt, but a week later, I asked Donnie to investigate before ending the relationship. He said, "Okay." I continued to pray for God's hand as he started to investigate and learn what this meant for him.

When Donnie wants to learn about something, he starts by talking with people he knows and trusts. First, he went to his doctor to understand the medical perspective. During their conversation, his doctor said, "Donnie, do you think I have it?" And Donnie said, "No, of course not."

"Well, I do... and I can tell you, as a physician, very few people tell their partner in a timely way so that you have a choice. If I were you, I would look at the fact that you have an honest woman here... and that's important."

Next, he went to the second person he wanted to talk to: his pastor. Pastor Bruce is someone he has known for a very long time, and Donnie wanted to get his spiritual perspective.

Donnie shared with Pastor Bruce about my situation and that he thought he couldn't stay in the relationship. Pastor Bruce looked at him and said, "Wow, Donnie, you are so lucky!" And Donnie responded, "Yeah, I can still get out of this."

Pastor Bruce said, "No, you are so lucky because she has to wear her sin on the outside of her body and must tell people. You get to wear your sin on the inside of your body, and you don't have to tell anyone. Brother, take the plank out of your eye. We all have sin!"

That caught Donnie by surprise, but he realized that it was true. He hadn't led a sinless life. None of us leads a sinless life.

The third person he went to was his mom. Oh, my. He loves his mama, and I love that he loves his mom. She is an incredible woman. When he told her the news, in her signature humor and perspective, she replied, "Son, it's a rash. Get over it!" And remember, she introduced us! And he was like, "Okay, it's done. God has clearly shown me His hand in this."

Closing

Through this experience, we learned that we all have sinned and that God's redeeming love can move us beyond our past and into love for Him and each other.

If you feel defined by the sin in your life or bad choices as I did, bring it to the foot of the cross. Jesus died for you and me so we would not be in bondage to our sinful nature.

If you haven't accepted His gift of freedom from sin, you can today. It's as simple as saying, "Jesus, I am a sinner. I believe You died for me to pay the penalty for my sins and rose again, and I now receive You as my Lord and Savior." He wants you to have that freedom, too. You only need to ask Him.

As I conclude, if the statistics in your life are not going as you want or you want to experience true freedom, turn them over to Jesus. He'll redefine them in His love and His grace. Thank you.

Richard's Story

Richard gave this testimony at a Men's Breakfast at his church for 100+ men. Because he was given a 30-minute timeframe, and he knew several people in the audience personally, he had some fun with this while still employing the L.O.V.E. guiding principles to keep his audience engaged. His grandsons also attended this event.

It's Never Too Late, and You Are Never Too Old!

Opening

Good Morning! I'm Richard Leonard, and I am honored and blessed to be here with you today.

How was the breakfast? A healthy choice of bacon, eggs, gravy, biscuits, and pancakes—is there a paramedic here?

It reminds me of a story.

An elderly couple admitted by St. Peter through the pearly gates found conditions were just heavenly. The man said to his wife, "I could have been here two years ago if you hadn't fed me all that oat bran!"

Seriously, Mark Twain was quoted as saying, "Eat a live frog first thing in the morning, and nothing worse will happen to you the rest of the day."

The table topics were interesting and let you know one another better. Let me ask you a question. What would you say if your table topic question asked you to share your testimony and how God was working in your life? How could you and I renew our sense of purpose and peace through fellowship, spiritual growth, and invitations to serve?

I want to share how I was called. To do that, I had to think and pray about the spiritual markers in my life. You know, those events that happened to you were not a coincidence—they were a God moment. A point in time where your life was changed—sometimes significantly—spiritually.

Called to conversion, called to transformation, called to faithfulness, and called to fruitfulness. And how this church and men like you helped me renew my sense of purpose and peace, to listen and to serve.

Let me give you some background!

Chapter 1

I'm a native Californian raised in North Hollywood and Orange County in a Catholic family. I started college in the 60s but didn't finish; I enlisted in the US Army.

I was commissioned as a second lieutenant in the infantry, went to flight school to become an Army Aviator, and went to Vietnam to fly UH1 helicopters in an air calvary troop, a combat unit. Every day was a new mission, and the circumstances led to a dampening of my spiritual walk. You know, you accept death even though you are living. Military humor allows you to suppress the real things that happen, and the spiritual markers made for you are not consistently recognized immediately. Here are some adages you may have heard that hide the fundamental truths.

- There are old pilots and bold pilots—but very few old, bold pilots.

- The Jesus nut—that big retaining nut on the top of the mast that keeps the rotor blades on a helicopter. If it comes off, you fly like a homesick brick, and some say you only have time to say one word—Jesus—before that sudden stop at the end of your fall.

- Fright time—Hours and hours of boredom punctuated by moments of sheer terror.

I survived! I came home to an ungrateful nation, treated with contempt, and found solace with my brother pilots and officers in the US Army Reserve. I was spiritually wounded and bleeding—but functioning.

Then, God changed my life one day. It all happened on a cross-country formation flight to Tucson, Arizona. I met up with an old friend who had arranged a blind date for me. It was there that I met this incredible young woman, Libby. We had a great time that night, and I flew the mission the following day and didn't see her again.

One year elapsed between our blind date and our second meeting, my friend's wedding. One year later, we were married in the church with all the blessings one could hope for. I realized this woman's true depth and love for me and Our Lord—I was blessed in abundance.

That's when I was called to convert to transformation and faith. Early in our marriage, we went to a Christian marriage encounter weekend. Those three days broke open the dam of darkness from my military experiences, and through my wife's love, I was born again in my faith in Jesus Christ.

Psalm 91 is every soldier's prayer. David was indeed that kind of man, a warrior and king. The first seven verses of Psalm 91:1-7 say it all:

"Those who live in the shelter of the Most High will find rest in the shadow of the Almighty. This I declare about the LORD: He alone is my refuge, my place of safety; he is my God, and I trust him. For he will rescue you from every trap and protect you from deadly disease. He will cover you with his feathers. He will shelter you with his wings. His faithful promises are your armor and protection. Do not be afraid of the terrors of the night nor the arrow that flies in the day. Do not dread the disease that stalks in darkness nor the disaster that strikes at midday. Though a thousand fall at your side, though ten thousand are dying around you, these evils will not touch you."

Chapter 2

Have you ever considered there are spiritual markers throughout our lives?

Have you looked at the life you led, thinking and praying about those points in time when you experienced a significant event or made an important decision? Can you see where the Lord Jesus Christ made it an experience that would influence your life on earth—and in heaven? In my Kingdom Journey, Our Lord put many trials in my life. For me, it was the near misses during my combat missions in Vietnam. It was the marriage encounter with my wife, Libby. It was the time my 3-year-old middle son was stricken with an infection that put him in ICU for three weeks. Death and the possibility of a crippled life for his future confronted us every day during those three weeks he was in the hospital. The blessings of our family and our friends from church, as well as all of their prayers, were answered with his healing.

I received another call, but one that was most distressing. One morning, as I was leaving the house to go to the Aviation Unit, my wife was waiting by the front door for me—crying and holding our son. She said, "I don't think you are going to come home." She was terrified of the near misses I'd had that year flying. I had to choose—a military career or a family. So, after 13 years with the military, I decided family was more important! I transitioned to a civilian career through personal drive, education, and the support and encouragement of my wife.

Family and career were my calling—my fruitful-ness.

I'm skipping several significant events in my career after leaving the military. The trials of a family man working full-time and getting an undergraduate degree in Information Systems and an MBA. The trials of getting a job when we were literally broke. The trials of moving into a new profession and career and being recruited by an international accounting firm. We moved to Cardiff-by-the-Sea in San Diego, where we found a great church and Christian friends, some of whom are with me today! Three wonderful sons spiced our marriage and life. My career transitioned from public accounting to founding and running my own company. Later, a client enticed me to join a major oil company. It involved a move from California to Arizona and later to Oklahoma.

Each move was a journey but also a storm that our Lord continually put in my life, and His calling was one that I did not fully understand and heed. I thought I knew my purpose, but He had other purposes for me far beyond my perspective.

As I grew closer to our Lord Jesus, I finally started to listen. I was called to serve and give more in the fruits of my time, talents, and resources at my church in Oklahoma. Mission trips to Mexico, serving as an elder, a trip to Israel, and working and leading church ministries started to fill my life with new directions and insights.

Do you hear calls like those? Do you reflect on your life and see the spiritual markers that were put in your journey? Your family? Witnessing to those you work with or associate with? Doing work for the body of Christ through your church, a ministry, or supporting your community?

I know! It's priorities! Work, family, recreation, church, and all those other events that fill your days and weeks to the point you don't have the time or energy.

I remember our trip to Israel in 2008—We sailed out of Tiberius on the Sea of Galilee early one morning. Suddenly, our boat got caught in a storm! In the early morning! Deck chairs were sliding to the rails, and one had a woman sitting in it. Deckhands saved her! It became another one of those spiritual markers Jesus put into my life. You know, those sometimes little but significant events that come into your life where you realize, "I think God just talked to me." In my case, it takes a 2 x 4 board of wood to get my attention and reflection.

Jesus asks us to go, and He puts conflict in our life—but He is with us to overcome our fears and, through faith, give us hope for ourselves and others.

Faithfulness without fear

Mark 4:35-40, NLT, says:

> "*As evening came, Jesus said to his disciples, 'Let's cross to the other side of the lake.' So they took Jesus in the boat and started out, leaving the crowds behind (although other boats followed). But soon, a fierce storm came up. High waves were breaking into the boat, and it began to fill with water. Jesus was sleeping at the back of the boat with his head on a cushion. The disciples woke*

him up, shouting, 'Teacher, don't you care that we're going to drown?'

When Jesus woke up, he rebuked the wind and said to the waves, 'Silence! Be still!' Suddenly, the wind stopped, and there was a great calm. Then he asked them, 'Why are you afraid? Do you still have no faith?'"

When I retired in June of 2010, our plans to travel and enjoy the third trimester of our lives were suddenly dashed when my wife was diagnosed with stage IV esophageal cancer. The shock of the news, the grief and consequences of the cancer treatments, the acceptance it was Stage IV and could not be cured, and the resolution to prolong her life challenged us to the breaking point. The faith we both needed to carry our spirits through this final path of life gave us the hope and determination to deal with life.

My effervescent wife was not done with living restricted by constant chemotherapy treatments. She wanted to celebrate the life Jesus gave her, visit her friends and family, and be closer to her sons. Two lived here in San Diego, and the third was in Oregon.

Again, the Lord called! Let's go to the other side! Just as suddenly, our Lord brought this new storm with a long journey in our lives. This time, it started with a Category V tornado that struck Joplin, Missouri. I told my wife how close that tornado was to where we kept our RV. She said, "I want to see my family and friends back home in California; let's pack up and travel." We prepared our house for rental. We soon leased it and loaded the RV for a very long trip. Trip plans included RV stops, refueling, setting up visits with friends and family, sightseeing locations, and arranging chemotherapy, and later, radiation treatments.

We traveled from north of Tulsa, Oklahoma, down to Ft. Worth, Texas, picked up a lifelong friend, and traveled across the US to San Diego. We would drive for four hours, then stop and stay for two days or more at each stop. The trip to San Diego took three weeks! We stayed for chemotherapy treatments in San Diego, visiting with our two sons and their families. Libby underwent chemotherapy treatments and dealt with the nausea and fatigue that accompanied the harsh treatment.

Then we traveled north through California into Oregon, taking another lifelong friend with us. Again, we would drive for four hours, then stop and stay for two days or more at each stop. It took us over a month to get to Gold Beach, Oregon. Other friends from California and Oregon traveled to join us.

Libby witnessed her life's journey and love for Jesus to everyone, especially those undergoing cancer treatments with her at the cancer centers. They were amazed at her zest for life and love for the Lord. They were encouraged and gained hope after hearing everything she was doing while they were trying to cope. She lived her life to the fullest! She taught me to do the same.

The RV became the "mother ship" while our friends stayed with us for days. They would explore the countryside during the day and return for evening celebrations and dinner. We started traveling north with our friends joining us at different times. We traveled to Washington and into Canada, then returned to California to get the results of the radiation treatments.

They were not successful; Libby had just a few months left.

Our time on the road and in the RV lasted more than a year, ultimately bringing us back to San Diego. Libby, my loving wife of 38 years and the mother of my three sons departed to be with Our Lord with all of us at her side in November, 2012.

Chapter 3

So here I was, back in San Diego, my wife of 38 years having just departed to be with Our Lord Jesus, and my sons asking me to stay near them. The last few years of our life together taught me the true meaning of the word "cherish." Now I was alone, grateful that she was now with the Lord, but grieving. I quickly found that I needed to help my sons through their grief. The Lord gave me a new calling, helping me deal with a new life without my wife.

I had raised my family in North County of San Diego, so I found a place and started attending Carlsbad Community Church. The men in the congregation opened their arms and hearts. I met Bill Hosmer and Alan Bergstedt right away. Their invitations connected me to Bill's military ministry. Alan was leading the Men of Encouragement men's ministry and was also a Partner in the Barnabas Group. I have also been helping Veterans Village's Stand Down event, supporting homeless veterans. The Lord was hitting me over the head again with callings.

Our Senior Pastor, Alvin Helms, offered me a one-on-one discipleship study using the Gospel-Centered Life as a study guide. I got involved with other church activities. I used my time, talents, and network to support and encourage the Men's Breakfasts, the huge week-long garage sale, a Mission trip to Costa Rica with the Free Wheelchair Mission, the military ministry at Camp Pendleton, meeting and feeding people experiencing homelessness through the Bread of Life mission, and I continued to support homeless Veterans in the Veterans' Village Stand Down events. I attended Saturday and Sunday morning Bible studies to gain more knowledge of the Word of God. Jesus's love and fellowship with like-minded Christians recharged my heart and soul.

How does God talk to you? Through Scripture? Through invitations from people you know? Through small group meetings or Bible studies? There are so many ways to listen with an open heart. Let me tell you how the Lord worked on me to get me involved with an incredible Christian ministry.

Chapter 4

One day, Alan Bergstedt invited me to a Barnabas Group meeting. I saw how the Kingdom works on earth and met ordinary-looking people who were incredible Christians who encouraged and elevated ministries to help the needy.

At a Barnabas Group meeting in 2014, I sat across a circular table from a man who looked very familiar. We both sensed recognition and walked up to each other at the break. Jim Peevey was that man, and I renewed our friendship and brotherhood with him in Christ after a 25-year pause from when we had gone to the same church in Encinitas. I'm honored to say Jim is a great friend and Christian brother. We still serve together in the Barnabas Group with many others, including Bill Carson, who is also here today.

So, what's the deal about the Barnabas Group? Why did I like it so much? Why did they approach me to become their co-managing partner in 2018?

We are Christian men and women who want to encourage and support Christ-centered non-profit organizations we call ministries. We give them our time, talents, networks, and resources.

We have quarterly Summits where we give vetted ministries time to share their story and seek help from more than a hundred Christian men and women. We also meet monthly in smaller group settings and offer seminars for ministry leaders and partners throughout the year.

Here is a high-level view of what we do in the Barnabas Group each year.

The quarterly meetings put four ministries in front of a large audience. We see the patchwork of the Kingdom at a Barnabas Group meeting because we see what the ministries are doing and share their fruitfulness with our partners. They attend different churches throughout San Diego. We focus on our partners and, through them and using their networks, the ministries— to date, over three hundred of them. Those who attend are introduced to other partners and the presenting ministries, where they are free to follow their passions and find their callings.

I can't talk about all three hundred ministries, but I can highlight a few known to many of you. Let me showcase a few.

Free Wheelchair Mission

Men of Encouragement at Carlsbad Community Church has supported the Free Wheelchair Mission for many years. The Barnabas Group helped that ministry grow out of a garage in Orange County over a decade ago. Our church has contributed over $64,000 or 850 wheelchairs since we set up the Carlsbad Community Church Men's Team.

We have gone on mission trips to Vietnam, Peru, and Costa Rica through mutual cooperation and callings. Additionally, the founder of the FWM was our keynote speaker at last year's mission dinner, which helped draw several people outside of the church to the fundraiser. God be praised!

Outside the Bowl

Outside the Bowl has set up commercial-grade super kitchens in Haiti, Mexico, South Africa, and Malawi. Several Carlsbad Community Church members attended their past fundraiser, and OTB also helped us with food bowls and other materials for our Chili Cook Off.

Legacy Coalition

Legacy Coalition started in 2016. Ministry leaders at Legacy Coalition received bountiful blessings of encouragement and support after their presentations at the Barnabas Group meetings in Orange County and San Diego. Several of us attended the Legacy Coalition Summit in 2019, attended by over 1,200 grandparents. Later, Carlsbad Community Church hosted simulcast Grandparenting Summits for two years, ending in 2022.

What should you focus on for a calling when considering your life journey? Do you find that your age is starting to focus your efforts? Are you getting caught up in the retirement culture?

Legacy Coalition's primary mission is to engage, educate, encourage, and provide resources to help churches equip grandparents to impact future generations to know, love, and serve Jesus. God has instructed us to disciple our grandchildren. All of us must be "intentional Christian grandparents," for Deuteronomy says:

> *"But watch out! Be careful never to forget what you yourself have seen. Do not let these memories escape your mind as long as you live! And be sure to pass them on to your children and grandchildren"* (Deuteronomy 4:9, NLT).

Chapter 5

The Lord blessed a good and faithful servant!

So you see how my life became committed to working for the Lord. I was a widower for nine years, and I thought my life was complete. One Sunday after church, I asked a long-time acquaintance from church to coffee for a purpose. I wanted a female companion for a Barnabas Group event. She was startled but accepted! We were both in a state of amazement when we were married in November 2022 in front of one hundred and sixty people and our blended family of thirty people. Yes, thirty! Twelve adult children and their spouses and sixteen grandchildren ranging from four to twenty-four years in age!

Needless to say, we are attempting to master being "intentional Christian grandparents." Ladona and I have renewed our life's callings. Ladona's callings are to encourage and support international missionaries and domestic ministries, and my callings are being refocused. First and foremost, our grandchildren! Then, empowering those who wish to bring the word of Jesus Christ and the message of hope and salvation to the children of North County—and the domestic USA.

Closing

I want to extend an invitation to you to renew your life's calling.

Look back at all your spiritual markers and pray. Look at Scripture in such a way that it helps you see how your spiritual markers are pointing a way for you.

Do you hear that voice that says, "Hey, want to go to the other side? Are you willing to go on that boat in the Sea of Galilee?"

You were converted, you were transformed, you are faithful, and you can be fruitful. Give your time, talents, networks, and resources to serve God!

My sincere invitation to you:

1. Be a grandparent who impacts your family with the Christian love and leadership your grandchildren want. They matter! They need

hope and to know you and Jesus love them and will always be with them. They are not alone!

2. Be a father to your sons and daughters, repair and strengthen family relationships, and show them your faith in Jesus Christ as Lord and Savior through your love and actions.

3. Use your church to strengthen Christian fellowship and spiritual growth and be deliberate on invitations to serve. If you know others who do not attend church, encourage them to join you.

4. Yes, working together does build God's kingdom.

Remember, it is never too late! Thank you.

Chapter 16

Your Story Matters, Time to Share It!

As we near the end of our journey together in *Your Story for God's Glory*, I want to leave you with an empowering truth: Your voice matters. It matters to God, and it certainly matters to the lives you are yet to touch with your faith story.

In the Christian community we are familiar with the word stewardship. This word often is associated with stewarding wisely your finances, time, talents, and resources. But have you considered stewardship in terms of your testimony?

Your testimony is a resource that God intends to use for His purposes to bless people. If you choose not to share your story and instead bury it (keeping it to yourself), you rob someone from hearing about Jesus' transforming love and grace in a way that only you can tell it.

It's never too late to steward your story!

We have learned from Richard's story that although he had shared his testimony along his life's journey, it was only recently that he became intentional to steward his story in a way that has greater impact for those he loves and cares about. At age 70+, Richard is now more active in sharing his faith story and living out a life in service to God.

I invite you to do as Richard has done, and become more intentional with stewarding your story for God's glory. By reading this book, you have taken an important step to gaining the knowledge and guidance to share your story with confidence, clarity, and impact.

As your story continues to unfold, see it as a gift to continue to open and share with others. Remember your story is unique to you. Your story is a precious gift from God, and it holds the power to touch hearts, transform lives, and glorify Him in ways that you can now imagine after reading the courageous stories of the real-life people in this book.

Let's look at how far you've come. Throughout this book, you've delved into the art of sharing your faith story with confidence, clarity, and impact. You've explored the L.O.V.E. guiding principles, each one designed to transform your storytelling and faith-sharing abilities. You've journeyed through real-life stories and examples, understanding that those who may have felt unequipped, much like yourself, still found the courage to share their faith and inspire others.

Now, as we close this chapter, reflect on the transformative journey you've been on.

- Remember the power of **Listening to God First**, inviting the Holy Spirit to guide your words and align your purpose with His divine plan for you and your listeners. Remember that it is all about His love and those you share with.

- Recall the importance of **Organizing Your Story**, allowing your story to flow in a way that engages the hearts and minds of your listeners, opening them to greater hope and faith in God the Father, His son Jesus, and the Holy Spirit.

- Embrace the significance of **Valuing Your Audience**, personalizing your story for them, and inviting them into God's bigger life-changing story.

- Finally, hold onto the courage of **Enjoying Sharing Confidently**, knowing that nervousness can be overcome and your unique style can shine as you share your faith.

The words from Paul to Philemon remind us that our faith is enriched, deepened, and made whole when we actively share it. It's not just about giving. It's about receiving a full understanding of every good thing we have in Christ through the act of sharing.

"I pray that you may be active in sharing your faith so that you will have the full understanding of every good thing we have in Christ" (Philemon 1:6, NIV).

This may be the end of the book, but it is just the start of what God has in store for you and your story. Don't let hesitation or doubt hold you back any longer. The world needs your voice—a voice that can touch hearts, transform lives, and glorify God. You have the tools, the knowledge, and the love within you to make a difference in the lives of those around you. You have the power to introduce them to Jesus through your story.

I challenge you to take the next step. Find the opportunities, large or small, to share your faith story. Whether it's with a friend, a neighbor or coworker, or a room full of people, remember that your story has the potential to encourage love, hope, and faith, allowing the Holy Spirit to change lives.

Be confident in the journey you've undertaken, and trust that God is with you every step of the way. He is planning to make kingdom ripples through you and your story.

Your voice matters. It's time to share your story and let it resonate with the hearts and minds of those who are waiting to hear it.

Together, let's continue to glorify God through the stories we share and the lives we touch.

> *"Lord, use me to expand the world's perception of You.*
> *You are limitless, and I make myself available to be used as*
> *Your ambassador in circles large and small. Send me."*
> Prayer by Marshawn Evans Daniels,[16]
> 100 Days of Believing Bigger

---

[16] Marshawn Evans Daniels. 100 Days of Believing Bigger Devotional Journal, published by DaySpring, 2020. Referenced prayer is from Day 85.

Acknowledgments

Writing this book has been an unexpected faith journey—it has been a challenging yet encouraging collaborative process. At each turn, just when I wanted to give up, God would place another faithful Christian like you on my path to remind me how important and rewarding it is to give God's glory a voice— our voice.

Thank you...

For modeling faith and courage in action: Ciara, Oscar, Laura, Richard Leonard, Kara Bresee, Ray Holt, Mike Conway, Erin Weidmann, Jim Fallen, Ruth Tolly, Jay and Shane Panther, Marcia Ramsland, Fares Abraham, and the hundreds of amazing people who participated in my workshops and coaching sessions. Your willingness to share your real-life experiences with transparency inspires us to step up and trust God with our own stories.

For shaping my perspective and strengthening my faith: Diane West, Maria Keckler, Laura Georgakakos, Lisa Newmeyer, Amy Larson, Bob Shank, Jim West, Chau Hoyt, Estha Madeira, Rechelle Conde-Nau, Amy DeFehr, Arlana Scola, Ron Flores, Dora Akietteh, Rick Warren, and Marshawn Evans Daniels. Your wisdom, conviction, and compassion have inspired and shaped my faith, work, and life.

For helping me cross the finish line: Barbara Barr at Impeccably Edited, Sarah Bartholomew, Mario Tamayo, Jill

Addison, Pam Farrel, Christine Shade, Liz Bagby, Curt Hensley, Terri Podlenski, Amy Gray, Ginger Choucair, Celeste Bradley, and Gaylen Smith-Osborn—for reading, proofreading, editing, providing feedback, and holding me accountable. Without your help, support, and contributions, this book would not be a reality.

Marcy Pusey, my publisher and friend. You held my hand and encouraged me as I struggled through five years of drafts and restarts—you taught me that God's timing is always perfect, that there is purpose in the waiting, and that God never intends for us to go it alone.

For believing—always: My beloved family—Donnie, Jordie, and sister Nancy—for believing, praying, encouraging, and walking with me—at every turn.

Nancy, your unwavering faith inspires me every day. Thank you for encouraging me to stay the course for the calling God put on my heart.

Jordie, being your mom is my greatest gift from God. You are beautiful, talented, independent, and kind. Your spirit and courage continue to inspire me.

Donnie, your love, support, and commitment to our family has created the solid foundation that gives us the ability to pursue all that God intends for us. Your encouragement to bring this work to fruition has made it possible. We succeed together!

For who I am, who I'm becoming, and what I'm able to do. God—my Savior, my Father, my friend, and my guide. May all I do be pleasing to you. Jesus. You are the author and perfecter of my story; may all the glory be Yours.

Appendix

Application Worksheets, Templates, and Action Steps

As our journey nears an end, your journey to sharing your faith story is just beginning. God has a purpose and a plan to make His love, mercy, and redeeming nature known through your story. What a gift to be able to participate with Him in making eternal kingdom ripples!

As you embrace stewarding your story for God's glory it becomes an opportunity to experience God's transforming power at a deeper level for yourself and then to be able to share that experience with others.

This section is designed to help you take what you have learned and to apply it by providing L.O.V.E. in Action worksheets and templates for each of the guiding principles, along with worksheets for the chapters focused on non-profit ministries and helping the next generation to embrace their stories.

As you work through these templates and action steps continue to seek the Holy Spirit's guidance for what is useful for your specific personality, situation, and listeners. These are meant to be a resource and pathway to continue the journey of developing and delivering your story with confidence, clarity, and impact.

Your Story Matters! May God bless you as you share your story for His Glory.

Additional resources can be found at www.kingdompresenters. com/book-resources.

Chapter 1: Who Do You Say I Am?

Points to Remember:

- We must first answer for ourselves, "Who is Jesus to me?" before we can confidently share who He is with others.

- We are each unique in our experience of Jesus, enabling us to connect His message of love and grace with specific people in our community in a way that resonates with them.

- Your story matters! God wants to make Himself known through you and your story.

Scriptures to Reference:

> *"Who do you say I am? Simon Peter answered,*
> *'You are the Christ, the Son of the living God'"*
> (Matthew 16:15-16, NIV).

> *"But in your hearts, set apart Christ as Lord.*
> *Always be prepared to give an answer to*
> *everyone who asks you to give the reason for*
> *the hope that you have. Do this with gentleness*
> *and respect"* (1 Peter 3:15, NIV).

Questions to consider:

- Who do you say Jesus is to you?

- Who needs to learn what is possible for themselves through what Jesus has made possible for you?

- Are you willing to allow God to use you and your story to make Himself known?

Actions to take:

1. Take time to reflect on your relationship with Jesus.

2. How might you describe that to someone? Consider some words, emotions, and outcomes that represent for you who He is. List a few here:

_____

_____

_____

_____

Chapter 2: Discovering God's Will for Your Story

Points to Remember:

- His words, His love, and His purposes are what allow your story to be heard.

- Begin your faith story preparation with prayer time to seek God's will and purposes for you, your listeners, and your story.

- Seek to stay in your prayer conversation with the Lord long enough to gain an understanding of His heart and will for your listener, the situation, and for you.

- After you have shared your story, ask God how it went. Eternal impact is not always evident right away on a human level.

Scriptures to Reference:

"This is the confidence we have in approaching God; that if we ask anything according to His will, He hears us" (1 John 5:14, NIV).

"But when He, the Spirit of truth, comes, He will guide you to all truth" (John 16:13, NIV).

"For the one whom God has sent speaks the words of God, for God gives the Spirit without limit" (John 3:34, NIV).

Questions to consider:

- Who is God prompting you to share your unique story with?

- How does God see that person, their heart, and situation?

- How might that change how you share your story?

Actions to take:

1. Set aside time to pray and seek God's guidance about sharing your unique story, and for your listeners to receive it.

2. If helpful, use the examples of questions below to get you started. Feel free to change the questions to suit your situation.

3. Begin to identify who in your community may resonate with your story of hope and grace.

4. Who is God bringing to your mind right now? Begin to pray for them and for an opportunity to share your story.

5. Keep this prayer journal page with your questions to the Lord available as you continue to prepare your story. Add to it as your story evolves.

Relationship Prayer Journal

Father, who would You like me to speak to about You?
Father, what part of my story would You like me to share with them?

Father, how can they best relate to You through me?

Father, what is Your heart for them?

Father, how can I serve my listeners best?

Father, is there a Scripture to reference?

Chapter 3: Why Organize Your Faith Story

Points to Remember:

- Organizing your story helps you and your listeners gain the most out of your testimony.

- Without proper organization, your story may become confusing, hindering the impact you can have on your listeners.

- Organizing your story is not meant to limit or confine you. Instead, it helps you keep focused and your listeners engaged so that the Holy Spirit can stir their souls as you speak.

Scripture to Reference:

"Pray that I may proclaim it clearly, as I should.
Be wise in the way you act toward outsiders; make the
most of every opportunity. Let your conversation be
always full of grace, seasoned with salt, so that you may
know how to answer everyone."
(Colossians 4:4-6, NIV).

Questions to Consider:

- What has been your response to a story that is confusing or not organized? Did it enhance or hinder your relationship with the storyteller?

- Do you feel confined when adding structure to your story? Have you considered that it may provide more flexibility in the moment?

- When has a story changed your perspective about something?

Actions to Take:

1. Reflect on the idea that organizing your story is an act of obedience. When God calls you to share your experiences, He doesn't just ask for your words. He asks for your heart, your commitment, and your willingness to honor His message.

2. Pray and let God know your intentions to honor that commitment.

Chapter 4: Map Your Spiritual Journey

Points to Remember:

- A spiritual autobiography is simply a way to look at how God has worked in and throughout your life. It is the charting of life events that have influenced who you are and God's influence and impact on your life.

- Mapping your faith journey helps you identify key events and turning points, enabling you to be intentional with describing Jesus and His influence within your story.

- Taking time to map out your story will help you find the unique parts of your story, and shape that into something meaningful for your listeners.

- Creating a map is the first step to being intentional with your story versus "winging it."

Scripture to Reference:

"Only be careful, and watch yourselves closely so that you do not forget the things your eyes have seen or let them slip from your heart as long as you live. Teach them to your children and to their children after them"
(Deuteronomy 4:9, NIV).

Questions to Consider:

- Is there a specific event or season of your life that reflects the turning point in your relationship with Jesus?

- When has your faith been tested or strengthened? Was it tied to an event, decision, or person?

- How has your relationship with Jesus evolved over time?

Actions to Take:

1. Set aside time to work on documenting your spiritual journey.

2. Map out your life story, focusing on the key events, issues, and influences in your life. Highlight the events along the way that had significant faith implications for you.

3. Identify key turning points for you and the emotions associated with them.

4. Begin to consider which of your key events, issues, or influences could become a 5-minute story that you can share to represent how Jesus is working in your life.

Use this timeline to map out your life story, focusing on the key events, issues, and influences in your life. Highlight the events along the way that had significant faith implications for you.

Chapter 5: Outline Your Story Elements

Points to Remember:

- When you begin with an outline, creating and delivering a cohesive story is much easier.

- Getting clear on your big-picture story elements before diving into the details is key to engagement and story flow.

- Organize your outline using four simple structure basics: Story Theme, Open, Body, Close.

- Using an outline versus a set script enables you to go "off-script" when prompted by the Holy Spirit.

- Creating an outline gives you a useful tool for practicing and as reference notes if needed.

Scripture to Reference:

> *"Rather, it is the Father, living in me, who is doing his work"* (John 14:10, NIV).

Questions to Consider:

- Can you think of more than one story to tell that represents Jesus' role in your faith journey?

- Have you identified two to three key points you want your listener to take away? Are they incorporated into your outline?

- How does having a "big-picture" view of your story help you to build confidence?

Actions to Take:

1. Identify an event or turning point for which you can now outline a five-minute testimony.

2. Consider whether you have two to three events or turning points you can tie together under one theme if given a longer timeframe?

3. Use the template below to organize your thoughts and create a draft outline of your story

Template: Your Story Outline

The Moral of Your Story: The driving theme and aspects of God's character you're highlighting
Opening: Transitioning into your story
Body of your story: 1st Chapter
Body: 2nd Chapter

Body: 3rd Chapter (Optional)

Close: Concluding your story

Chapters 6–10: Bring Your Story to Life

Points to Remember:

- A relevant story is compelling. Consider your listeners' interests, personality, concerns, and spiritual awareness as you prepare your story.
- Keep in mind that each of the structure elements has a purpose:
    - o Your theme creates focus for you and your listeners.
    - o The opening provides context and engagement.
    - o The body helps bring to life the story while maintaining a cohesive storyline.
    - o The close invites your listeners into God's bigger story and/or the next natural step.
- Strive to share enough details to bring your story to life without distracting or confusing your listeners with too much information.

Scripture to Reference:

"We are, therefore, Christ's ambassadors as though God were making his appeal through us. We implore you on Christ's behalf: Be reconciled to God" (2 Corinthians 5:20, NIV).

Questions to Consider:

- What do you want your audience to think about or focus on most about God?
- When adding details to your story, ask yourself if the detail is necessary or could it create a distraction?

- When it comes to story structure elements, what have you seen or experienced as a listener that you found most helpful?

Actions to Take:

1. Go back to the outline you created and add in the pertinent details that fill out your story and bring it to life. Remember, the goal is not to be "scripted" but to have a good sense of what you would want to say when you share your story.

2. Talk through the draft you created with a Christian mentor, friend, or family member. Ask them to assist you in eliminating details to be more concise. Ask them what resonated with them, what was not clear, and what information did not seem relevant. Keep an open mind about their feedback. Adjust accordingly.

Chapter 11: Personalize Your Story for Your Audience

Points to Remember:

- The power of personalization is in making your story relevant to your listeners.

- Personalizing your story for your audience can be simple: incorporate questions, use inclusive language, recognize them and their situation, and invite them into God's bigger story.

- Jesus modeled these ways of personalizing in His interaction with the woman at the well (John 4:4-26, NIV).

Scripture to Reference:

"With stories like these, He presented His message to them, fitting the stories to their experience and maturity" (Mark 4:33, MSG).

Questions to Consider:

- Is your tendency to be more one-sided or two-way when sharing your story?

- Which of the four engagement tools are you most comfortable with?

- Would you be comfortable with adding the other tools, if appropriate, for your listeners?

- Have you considered what the next natural steps could be for your listeners? Are you ready to extend an invitation to know Jesus, if appropriate?

Actions to Take:

1. Go back and personalize your story draft for your intended listeners. Consider where you could integrate some of the engagement tools: questions, inclusive language, something you know of them, and an invitation to bring your listeners into the bigger story.

2. Review your story from your audience's perspective and consider what would feel relevant to them. If you are not sure, pray and ask the Holy Spirit to guide you.

Chapter 12: The Five P's that Lead to Confidence

Points to Remember:

- Nervousness is normal!

- The Five P's help you gain confidence:

    o Prayer: His Strength, His Love, His Outcomes.

    o Preparation: It's a process; plan on revisions.

    o Practice: Frees you up to be you. Out-loud practice is best.

    o Proactive: Be proactive with nervous symptoms.

    o Presence: Be real versus perfect—that's what connects!

- Embrace your unique style and personality, allowing God to use it for His purposes.

Scriptures to Reference:

"The One who calls you is faithful, and He will do it"
(1 Thessalonians 5:24, NIV).

"So do not throw away your confidence; it will be richly rewarded. You need to persevere so that when you have done the will of God, you will receive what He has promised" (Hebrews 10:35–36, NIV).

"You did not choose me. I chose you.
I appointed you to go and produce lasting fruit"
(John 15:16, NIV).

Questions to Consider:

- What personality trait, something unique, or situation are you undervaluing that God wants to use to make Himself known?

- Do you expect yourself to be perfect when sharing your story?

- Has that prevented you from sharing in the past?

- What is one step of faith and courage you could take today?

Actions to Take:

1. Schedule time to practice saying your story out loud.

2. Consider videotaping yourself with your mobile phone. Signs of nervousness that we think are visible usually are not. Honestly assess whether nerves are apparent.

3. Identify what stands in your way of sharing your story (fear, unprepared, etc.).

4. Pray for God to show you ways to move past any barrier and gain greater confidence.

Chapter 13: Encouraging the Next Generation

Points to Remember:

- When we encourage the next generation to share their faith with their own authentic voice and within their own style, they can speak with confidence and transparency in a way that has an impact on their generation and beyond.

- Every voice has Kingdom value and impact no matter the age, personality, or background.

- God has given this next generation their own unique stories to make Himself known.

Verse to Reference:

> *"Don't let anyone look down on you because you are young, but set an example for the believers in speech, in life, in love, in faith, and in purity"* (1 Timothy 4:12, NIV).

Question to consider:

- How could you encourage the next generation to embrace and share their own stories?

Actions to take:

1. If you have young people in your life, begin by asking them about themselves (hobbies, what they have learned recently, favorite subjects, etc.). The idea is to help them start to reflect on what they care about and how that shapes who they are and their story. As you listen be

careful to not direct them or judge them, just allow them to share and be heard.

2. Share that God has given each of us a story that can make a difference for someone else, no matter our age, personality, or background.

3. Consider sharing with them the L.O.V.E. principles as they embrace their own story—or share how the L.O.V.E. principles helped you to organize and share your own story.

Chapter 14: Deliver a Compelling Ministry Partnership Story

Points to Remember:

- Key supporters, donors, and advocates often start as audience members attending an event to learn about the ministry.

- Create connections with them by delivering a clear and compelling *partnership* story.

- Weave volunteer stories into your ministry story to demonstrate partnership in action.

- Address your supporters' inherent questions to help them to determine their participation level.

- God is the ultimate provider who moves the mission forward.

Verses to Reference:

> *"Now to each one, the manifestation of the Spirit is given for the common good"*
> (1 Cor. 12:7, NIV).

Questions to consider:

- What questions would you want answered to invest your personal time, talents, or resources? (These are probably similar to your audience's questions for your ministry)

- What story are you already sharing of those whom you serve? Where can you now add the volunteers' side of the story to reflect the partnership in action?

Actions to take:

1. Pull out and review the last ministry presentation you gave or a draft of the ministry story you are currently working on.

2. Look at your ministry presentation through the lens of finding the "Sweet Spot" between God's story, your ministry story, and the audience's story. How have you represented each of these?

    *   God's Story: Where has God opened doors for the ministry or you? How is Jesus becoming known to those you serve?

    *   Your Ministry Story: Is it clear who you serve and why that matters? Is it clear what the ministry needs to move forward? Is there a plan and/or approach in place?

    *   Audience's Story: How can your audience members make a specific difference with their time, talents, networks, or resources? Is it clear what partnership/volunteering looks like with your ministry?

Small adjustments can go a long way to helping your audience to see themselves helping you move the ministry mission forward. By reflecting on finding the sweet spot for your ministry story can make a big difference to your audience' engagement.

Endnotes

1. Mark Batterson, lead pastor and author. Quote referenced from his posting on Vimeo.com, November 7, 2017.

2. Lisa Newmeyer, prayer coach and founder of Breakthru2u. For more information contact: lisa@breakthru2u.com.

3. Maria Keckler, Ph.D. *Bridge Builders: How Superb Communicators Get What They Want in Business and Life. New York:* Morgan James, 2016.

4. Dr. Dora Akietteh, *Heart of Prayer* workshop; November 15, 2022, San Diego, CA.

5. Rick Warren Blog: *Communicating More Like Jesus: part 4*. June 3, 2022.

6. Author Spencer Johnson, M.D. in his book *Peaks and Valleys; Making Good And Bad Times Work For You—At Work And In Life.* Simon & Schuster, 2009.

7. Bob Shank,. founder of Priority Living and The Master's Program. www.priorityliving.org.

8. Marcy Pusey, CRC, CTRP, trauma counselor, and author of *Overcoming Writer's Block: The Writer's Guide to Beating the Blank Page.* Fresno, CA: Miramare Ponte Press, 2022.

9. Brian Solis, author, speaker, futurist. Quote accessed from Instagram, August 16, 2020.

10. Sarah Young. *Jesus Calling*, published by Thomas Nelson, 2008. Reference from October 31 devotional page.

11. The study led by Microsoft Canada on how technology has affected attention spans was conducted in 2015. Sourced through Google on April 30, 2024.

12. Sam Horn. *Got Your Attention: How to Create Intrigue and Connect with Anyone*, 2015. LinkedIn article: "Why Every Speaking Opportunity Matters," accessed September 20, 2017.

13. Rick Warren. *The Purpose Driven Life*: Zondervan 2002, page 277.

14. The 2023 Asbury Revival. Wikipedia. Accessed April 9, 2023.

15. The Barnabas Group: San Diego and Orange County groups. www.sandiego.barnabasgroup.org.

16. Marshawn Evans Daniels. 100 Days of Believing Bigger Devotional Journal, published by DaySpring, 2020. Referenced prayer is from Day 85.

www.ingramcontent.com/pod-product-compliance
Lightning Source LLC
Chambersburg PA
CBHW051133120626
46547CB00012B/786